MARCUS AURELIUS

THE DIALOGUES

MARCUS AURELIUS

THE DIALOGUES

ALAN STEDALL

SHEPHEARD-WALWYN (PUBLISHERS) LTD

First published in 2005 by
Shepheard-Walwyn (Publishers) Ltd
15 Alder Road
London SW14 8ER

Reprinted 2007

British Library Cataloguing in Publication Data
A catalogue record of this book
is available from the British Library

ISBN-13: 978-0-85683-236-9
ISBN-10: 0-85683-236-7

Typeset by Alacrity,
Sandford, Somerset
Printed through SS Media Ltd, Wallington, Surrey
Jacket artwork by Andrew Candy

To undertake our work on hand in accordance with what we know to be right, with enthusiasm, manfully and with kind-heartedness. In this pursuit we should allow no lesser issues to distract us, but instead preserve our spirit pure and upright, as if at the next moment we might have to return it Him who gave it. If we take this position firmly, expecting nothing and avoiding nothing, but instead remaining content simply that we have conducted ourselves in accordance with what we know to be right, and with truthfulness with our fellow man, then this is the path to a happy life, and there is no man or god who can prevent us from following it.[1]

Marcus Aurelius, Roman Emperor, AD 121-180

High glory of the company of heaven,
Lord of the manifold name,
Eternal and everlasting is Thy power!

Blessed be Thou
O great Architect of Creation,
Ordering all things in the ways of Thy laws!

To call upon Thy name
Is meet and right for mortal kind,
For we are born of Thyself:
Yea, and to us, to us alone
Of all that lives and moves upon the earth,
Is granted a voice and an utterance.

Therefore now will I sing praises unto Thee!
Therefore now and for ever glorify Thy power![2]

Hymn of Cleanthes, Stoic Philosopher, 331-231 BC

Dedicated to
the memory of my father and mother,
Joseph and Freda Stedall

CONTENTS

PUBLISHER'S NOTE

MARCUS AURELIUS (AD 121-180) was the last of the 'five good Roman Emperors' and is famous for his classical philosophical notes, *Meditations,* written while on his many military expeditions.

On coming to the throne in 161, at the age of forty, Marcus inherited the responsibility for an Empire that was at once the greatest the world had ever known and, at the same time, teetering on the brink of collapse. Over the next nineteen years, up to his death in 180, he lead a series of successful military campaigns to defend the borders of the Empire. He thereby preserved Roman civilization and world culture for a further generation.

A man of considerable depth and learning, Marcus combined the duties of the palace and battlefield with his continuing love for and pursuit of philosophy. For the first and last time, Rome had an Emperor whose rule was based on benevolent philosophical principles: something akin to Plato's ideal of the philosopher king.

Contempories of Marcus show due respect and admiration for him as a man, who, although never physically strong, resolutely faced up to the immense responsibilities and personal adversities that fell upon him, and who unstintingly discharged the duties of his position fairly and reasonably. Marcus remained modest, charitable, undaunted and true to his principles to the very end.

The notes that Marcus jotted down for his own spiritual refreshment in *Meditations* provide an insight into the pre-Christian core beliefs and principles that sustained him against all odds. *Meditations* consists of twelve books of 488 individual notes, but, of their nature, they lack overall coherence or a sequential development of thought.

In 168 Marcus and his brother through adoption, Lucius, met with the famous Hellenic surgeon of antiquity, Galen, and an Egyptian high priest of Isis, Harnouphis, at Aquileia on the Adriatic coast.

In this book Alan Stedall recasts the essence of *Meditations* so as to portray a philosophical discussion and debate between these three famous figures of the classical world. In doing so he brings to life the underlying ethos of Marcus Aurelius in dialogue form which allows Marcus to expound and defend his Stoic beliefs. Thus *The Dialogues* depict not only Marcus's kernel beliefs, but also the essential character of the man that gave rise to them.

The Dialogues offer the reader a clear and coherent set of pre-Christian humanistic principles, founded not on any obligation to believe in supernatural events or beings, nor on any threat or promise of eternal damnation or salvation, but on a universal, rationally based spirituality.

INTRODUCTION

IT WAS AFTER nineteen years as a Roman Catholic that I found myself progressively uneasy with my faith. That is not to say that the Faith itself had changed; neither had my admiration for many of its celebrants and devotees, whom I continued to find exemplary in their charitable nature, warm-heartedness and liberal outlook. My difficulty arose in my inability to continue to accept certain fundamental beliefs of Christianity.

Specifically, I found increasing difficulty in stating that I believed in life after death; that Jesus was God; that he had performed miracles; that he had been incarnated as the result of an immaculate conception and had risen from the dead. Clearly this is not a short or trivial list of objections to the orthodox Christian faith.

For some years I convinced myself that, although I held these aspects of the faith to be at best unlikely, if not downright impossible, my active participation in the Church was justified because of the manifest benefits of the moral teachings and ethical way of life it promoted.

In truth, I had some difficulty with the Church's obsession with things sexual: its concern that its members should not use contraceptives; should not practice homo-sexuality; should not have sex outside of marriage; and that its priests must remain celibate and could not be female. I saw these as unnatural and unhealthy intrusions into personal matters that were nothing to do with vital spirit-ual issues, and, of themselves, had little to do with morality. To be fair, while I found this peculiar obsession puzzlingly bizarre and medieval, it did not impact upon me personally.

But I did find that reciting *The Credo*, confirming my belief in the miracles I questioned, was becoming increas-ingly difficult. At first I attempted to convince myself that this was unimportant, that such statements of belief were ritualistic and not to be taken literally in this modern scientific age.

But my discomfort became intolerable when I began to realise that, in reciting the statements in *The Credo*, I was undermining my own sense of integrity, and was basing my faith on an underlying self-deceit. I concluded that, no matter how highly I prized the spiritual, moral and social values of the Christian faith, for me such highly desirable ends could not justify a means that involved self-deceit: a personal faith not based on honesty and truth to oneself is not a faith at all.

This is not to say that I felt in any way disparaging of Christian ethics. From my own perspective, if Jesus had been 'only' a man and had consequently died fully and finally for his beliefs set out in the Gospels, then I find this to be even the more admirable than the orthodox Christian view of him as God who was subsequently resurrected. As a mere mortal man, he would have made the final and ultimate sacrifice to become the living (and dying) embodiment of Gandhi's exhortation to 'be the change you wish to see in the world'.

For my own part, I felt no need of the promise of an after-life to justify my attempts to live the best life that I could in the here and now. Indeed, the promise of a heaven, and threat of a hell, were not only superfluous, they actually contaminated virtuous attempts at moral behaviour by suggesting that this could be achieved only through a set of external (and eternal) promises and threats. From my perspective it seemed that leading the good life, or even the valiant pursuit of it, was in fact its own reward; otherwise one would have to conclude that man was, of his nature, essentially evil and could only be coerced onto a moral path by divine intervention. The experiences of my fellow men taught me that this was not so.

So I cast myself adrift from Christianity, from its valued community, its safe harbour of belief and the peace of mind that the faith offers.

An atheistic position, however, was not the alternative destination I sought. The concept of a life and cosmos without purpose is one I find fundamentally obscene. It

implies that the human race is trapped and condemned to
suffer pointlessly in the mindless mechanism of a vast
emotionless and purposeless cosmic machine – the final
outcome of all the strivings, sufferings and achievements of
our species over the millennia being reduced to no more
than detritus in space by some accidental collision with a
passing asteroid.

I read Don Cupitt and tried to get to grips with his
attempts to construct a 'post-religion religion', but concluded that this was an intellectual fudge, requiring us to
believe in a God while at the same time acknowledging that
he was dead. I don't believe He is.

I also dabbled in the teachings of certain Eastern
religions but found the underlying concepts – of detaching
oneself from the material world and accepting life fatal-
istically – to be too defeatist for my taste. In my view we do
not come to terms with, let alone make the best of, this
thing called life by detaching ourselves from it. Even in the
darkest of interpretations, life at the very least appears to
offer us a short vacation from oblivion. In my view life is
to be lived.

What I sought was a set of life-engaging, coherent
humanistic precepts based on a spiritual belief that did not
require miraculous foundations or divine coercion.

Meditations

IT WAS THEN that I read Marcus Aurelius's *Meditations*, translated by Maxwell Staniforth. Here was a historic, real figure who had tried his best to live by essentially pre-Christian Stoic principles and, it seems, had largely succeeded. He didn't give up his belief in God or gods; he wasn't sure whether there was a life after death, but concluded that this shouldn't in any case influence his behaviour in this life. The philosophy that he espoused was one of active and vigorous engagement with life, with the overall objective of improving the physical and spiritual lot of his fellow man.

The Stoic philosophy on which many of Marcus's beliefs were based was founded upon the intellectual lineage of great Greek philosophers such as Socrates, Plato and Cleanthes. However, Marcus's personal belief-set was not purely Stoic: it was heavily biased by, and overlaid with, strong humanistic beliefs. His was not a cold-hearted and detached Stoicism; it was, above all, kindly, cheerful, understanding and forgiving of his fellow man. Contrary to the traditional teachings of Stoicism, Marcus unashamedly grieved the loss of those he loved as much as any other man.

It was in Staniforth's translation that I found the germ of the belief system I was seeking. However, the *Meditations* is essentially, and unapologetically, a set of personal notes jotted down by Marcus Aurelius, on his many military expeditions, for his own spiritual refreshment. Indeed, the simple and original title for these notes was *To Myself* and it is doubtful that he ever intended them to be read by other eyes. They are not, they do not set out to be, a set of moral teachings. Nonetheless, Staniforth's excellent translation captures not only the personal thoughts and sharp self-criticism of Marcus Aurelius, it portrays his thoughts in an almost poetic form that adds force to their impact.

The fragmentary nature of the *Meditations* can be likened to the shards of a beautiful Grecian urn: each shard is beautiful when examined on its own, but the curious mind desires to know what coherence and beauty they might portray if re-assembled into some semblance of the original artefact.

I could find no work that attempted to do this. I read *The Spiritual Teachings of Marcus Aurelius* by Mark Forstater but was disappointed to find that it seemed as if all he had done was modernise the notes in the *Meditations*, then sort them mechanically into an order of contemporary applicability. This did not offer the overall coherence I was seeking; moreover, much of Marcus's personal style of writing and thinking had been lost. I felt that understanding the character of the man was almost as important as understanding the beliefs that his character had given rise to.

The Dialogues

THIS BOOK is my attempt to construct a largely coherent vessel from the beautiful shards of thinking that Marcus Aurelius left us. I openly confess that I have added to his own ideas where I felt the vessel I was attempting to assemble had essential pieces missing.

In particular, those passages describing the drive to seek meaning in life are wholly my own. I felt them to be fundamental to Marcus's philosophy as they attempt to answer the question that, to his credit, would probably never have occurred to Marcus regarding the underlying need for philosophical engagement in the first place: 'Why bother?'

In the final chapter I try to crystallise what I take to be Marcus's kernel philosophical belief. In doing this I certainly step beyond the various hints that he leaves us, to make his statement of faith more explicit.

On the other hand, I admit that a vast number of 'shards' have not found a place in my artefact. The *Meditations* leaves one spoilt for choice as to which of the 488 individual notes that Marcus left us in his twelve books should be incorporated into a work such as this. Inevitably a re-composer of Marcus's belief system has an end-view in mind and selects elements on this basis.

I chose to adopt a dialogue form for this work for three vital reasons.

Firstly, this form is traditional for philosophical works since it enables the development of rationale and argument with some degree of literary energy, and avoids the risk of becoming too dry.

Secondly, the dialogue structure enables Marcus's views to be represented in a simple, logical sequence that allows a more coherent construction of his position than may be found in the *Meditations*. It is my hope that his belief system may thus be more accessible, and may benefit a wider readership than the more precise and necessarily more academic direct translation.

Thirdly, I myself yearned to hear Marcus openly express and defend his own beliefs. Not finding this in any other work, I determined that the only way to meet my need was to construct the necessary stage myself.

The three characters I have depicted in dialogue with Marcus – his adopted brother, Lucius, the celebrated classical anatomist of the ancient world, Galen, and the Egyptian high priest of Isis, Harnouphis – are real historical figures, as is the main narrator, Bassaeus Rufus, Praetorian Prefect to Marcus. They really did meet at Aquileia on the Adriatic coast in 168. Did they engage in a dialectical discussion such as I have presented? We will never know. However, given Marcus Aurelius's passion for philosophy, and its traditional development through dialectical discussion, I like to think he would not have missed the opportunity, given the celebrated nature of his guests.

Marcus Aurelius summarised his general attitude to life as 'more like wrestling than dancing', because 'life demands a firm and watchful stance against any onset.'[3] This seems a somewhat stern and unfashionable view of life from the perspective of the upbeat cultural zeitgeist of Western life in the twenty-first century. It therefore requires some explanation of the circumstances in which Marcus found himself that caused him to take this view of life.

Marcus Aurelius

MARCUS WAS BORN in 121, into a position of privilege within a wealthy Roman family. By this time Rome had expanded into the largest empire the world had ever known, absorbing and assimilating Hellenistic and Egyptian cultures. The Empire was highly organised and centrally controlled. However, its weakness lay in the extent of its expansion. The borders now extended to Britain in the west, Germany in the north, Syria in the east and North Africa in the south: this was a truly vast area to manage, especially given the primitive methods of transport and communication at the time. More importantly, simple geometry dictated that the expansion of territory had vastly increased the length of borders that had to be garrisoned, to prevent local invasions from adjoining nations and tribes, jealous of Rome's power and wealth.

In effect, the past military triumphs of Rome had led to the growth of an empire that was now so large that defending the conquered territories was a military and administrative task of Herculean proportions. Although the central territories that had been occupied were relatively peaceful, Rome was teetering on the brink of losing control of its borders.

During Marcus's lifetime great events were to occur, some natural (such as the catastrophic plague of 166) and some man-made (for example the rebellion of the Roman legions based in Egypt in 175), that would push the unstable Empire almost past the tipping-point.

Both of Marcus's parents died when he was young and it fell to his grandfather to raise him. As a young man his serious and scholarly ways greatly impressed the Emperor Hadrian, who nicknamed him 'Verissimus',[4] 'truest'. It seems that Hadrian had early identified Marcus as a possible future successor, and consequently ensured that his upbringing and education were second to none.

In 138 Aelius Verus, Hadrian's chosen successor, predeceased Hadrian. Disappointed, and tired of life, Hadrian determined to die. Since Marcus was then still only seventeen, Hadrian adopted Marcus's uncle, Antoninus, as his successor on the understanding that Antoninus would, at the same time, declare Marcus as his own successor and that Antoninus also adopt the seven-year-old son of Aelius Verus, Lucius. Marcus thereby gained Lucius as a younger 'brother'. These arrangements were duly carried out and Antoninus became Emperor, being honoured by the Senate of Rome with the title 'Pius', reflecting his deep religious convictions and sense of duty.

Describing his uncle Antoninus, Marcus paints a picture of a man who was dedicated, modest and courteous. Certainly Marcus enjoyed a warm relationship with his uncle, who saw to Marcus's further education in philosophy, the classics and oratory. On Antoninus's death, at the age of seventy-five in 161, Marcus became Emperor when he was forty.

He accepted the throne reluctantly and only on condition that the Senate appoint his adopted brother, Lucius, as co-Emperor alongside him. There was no precedent for rule by joint Emperors and there certainly had been no obligation on Marcus to force the issue on the Senate. The action demonstrates Marcus's clear intention to commence his reign as he meant to go on: by acting in accordance with what he held to be right and fair, even when this was in no way demanded or expected of him.

It must be noted that the appointment of Lucius was a bad political move, given his weak nature. He turned out to be an ineffectual leader whose military successes in Syria and Alexandria were won purely on the backs of his generals.

Marcus's nineteen years in office – to his death in 180 – were marked by a series of major crises, each one of which he overcame through prompt attention and engagement.

In his position of absolute power, but accompanied by absolute responsibility, it was Marcus's avowed intention to preserve and protect the Empire he had inherited. He applied himself to this task conscientiously and whole-heartedly.

The preceding rule of his uncle had been marked by military neglect. Marcus therefore inherited a number of external threats to the Empire that came to a head during his reign but had been in gestation a long time previously.

In 161, the same year of Marcus's ascendancy, the Parthian Empire invaded the eastern borders of the Roman Empire. To drive them out Marcus had to bring legions from as far afield as the Danube, weakening defences there against the menacing Germanic tribes to the north. It took five years of bitter fighting to subjugate the Parthians; only then could the legions from Germany return home. When they did, in 166, they brought with them the plague.

In 169 major fighting occurred on the Hungarian plain. Military resources were now so short, following the plague, that gladiators and bandits were conscripted into special units, and property from the Imperial Palace was auctioned to fund military expenses.[5]

In 170 Germanic tribes invaded the northern borders of the Empire, crossing the Danube and destroying a Roman army of 20,000 men. At the same time a further army of barbarians attacked the Balkans: Greece was invaded, fol-lowed by Italy itself, the latter for the first time in hundreds of years.[6] It was only by leading his troops in person that Marcus was able to halt and turn these twin tides of invasion.

This Roman success, however, was followed by further enemy incursions, this time by the Moors into Spain. Forces were now withdrawn from Greece to counter this new invasion.

In 172 Marcus was required to put down a rebellion in Egypt, while once again countering new invasions by Germanic tribes from across the Danube. This latest Danubian war lasted a further three years.

In 175 Avidius Cassius, the Roman governor of Syria and 'dear friend' of Marcus, declared himself Emperor, supposedly on the false news of Marcus's death. Cassius then led the legions under his command in Syria and Egypt into open rebellion against Rome, causing panic there. Fortunately Marcus was able to retain the loyalty of his more powerful Danubian legions and, when news spread that he was still alive and about to move against Cassius, the latter was slain by his own officers. Nonetheless, Marcus felt obliged to take a tour of Palestine, Egypt and Greece to understand at first hand the level of internal unrest there.

When Marcus returned to Rome in 176 it was after eight years' absence in the field and he was welcomed as a hero.

In 178 Marcus left Rome for the last time, together with his son, Commodus, once more to face the threat of invasion by Germanic tribes from across the Danube. It is reported that many fellow philosophers were so concerned for Marcus's safety that they gathered together to clamour against his departure.[7] Their concern was justified: Marcus was to die, possibly from the plague, two years later in an encampment on the Danube, a month before he would have turned fifty-nine.

It is clear that Marcus tackled the unrelenting stream of threats to the Empire with energy, enthusiasm and an outstanding sense of duty. He spent most of his time, not in the Imperial Palace in Rome, but in military camps on the borders of the Empire, leading and directing his troops at first hand. Through sheer dint of extreme effort, he won the Empire a reprieve for more than a generation from its eventual demise, probably at the cost of his own health.

It would be difficult to overstress the gravity of Marcus's responsibilities during this period. Rome was the sole custodian of Western civilisation's most treasured achievements in the arts, sciences, engineering, philosophy, law and political theory (much of this garnered from the Hellenistic civilisation). The preservation of Rome was, for Marcus, not just the defence of his homeland and its culture, but the preservation of world civilisation itself against the threat of a return to barbarity. With the destruction of the Roman Empire, that occurred after the death of Marcus, Europe was to enter a period of cultural darkness, bloody wars, religious intolerance and persecutions that retarded progress in the arts and sciences for over a thousand years.

Marcus's personal life was also not free of trouble. His wife Faustina bore him fourteen children but he suffered the grief of seeing not less than seven of them die in early childhood. His only son to survive into adulthood, whom Marcus was obliged to appoint his successor (the only alternative under Roman law would have been to have the boy killed), was an increasing trial to him, displaying worsening fits of bad temper and ill-will. It is reported that, as a boy, Commodus once lost his temper with a bath-keeper who had allowed his bathwater to become lukewarm. In the absence of his father, Commodus ordered that the situation be corrected by the bath-keeper himself being thrown into the furnace.[8]

On succeeding to the throne, Commodus survived his father by just twelve years. Having become a hated, insane despot, he was assassinated by a wrestling companion who strangled him to death.

Marcus praises 'the artless and loving nature' of his wife, Faustina, and grieved her death, never subsequently remarrying or taking a mistress. However, persistent rumour had it that she had been unfaithful to Marcus on more than one occasion and that Commodus was not Marcus's son, but rather the result of a tryst between Faustina and a celebrated gladiator. Moreover, in 175

Faustina was said to have personally inveigled Avidius
Cassius to lead the rebellion in Egypt that threatened to
usurp Marcus. All letters in the possession of Cassius were
conveniently destroyed on his death when the rebellion
failed; these might well have included correspondence
from Faustina that would have implicated her in the rebellion.[9] Faustina died in 175, possibly by her own hand on
learning the news of the failure and death of Cassius.

Against such a background, the reader will hopefully
acknowledge that Marcus's view of life, as being 'more like
wrestling than dancing, since life demands a firm and
watchful stance against any onset',[10] was very realistic,
and indeed generous, considering his heavy responsibilities
and personal trials.

After the death of Marcus, the Roman Empire was to
enter a protracted period of unrest, characterised by a rapid
succession of rulers, each of whom came to office by vio-
lently usurping the position of his predecessor. The vitality
and strength of Rome's military capability was increasingly expended in internal political struggles. As her ability to
fend off external enemies drained away, the demise of the
Empire became inevitable. The moral is clear: a strong
nation has to be based on an internal political mechanism
that is widely accepted as fair, reasonable and just. Once
such broad acceptance is lost, a nation rapidly becomes
divided against itself and is easy prey to external aggressors:
'a house divided against itself cannot stand'.

This was perhaps Rome's fundamental weakness: its inability to sustain a republic and create a democracy sufficiently robust to defend itself against the challenges of emerging military dictatorships. In the absence of such sustainable and enduring political mechanisms, power fell into the hands of strong, charismatic rulers who commanded the loyalty of one or more of Rome's armies. From the reign of Nerva through to that of Marcus (AD96 to AD180), Rome was fortunate in its 'five good rulers'. At this period Rome is generally regarded as being at the zenith of its power and culture. But its luck ran out disastrously when Marcus's supposed son, Commodus, ascended the throne.

Marcus himself had delivered stability for over a generation to the populations of an empire that stretched over two thousand miles east to west. More importantly, he delivered it through a relatively benign and liberal rule. Arguably his only, though vital, omission was his failure to reform the political mechanisms of Rome so that succession did not depend on the potluck of bloodline, increasingly challenged by dagger and sword. However, given the continuous demands on Marcus simply to hold back Rome's enemies from its borders, perhaps even this criticism is unfair.

Marcus's unflinching sense of public duty and dedication won him the unqualified admiration of his contempories: Cassis Dio said after his death: 'He did not have the good fortune that he deserved, for he was not physically strong, and for almost his whole reign was involved in a series of troubles. But I for my part admired him all the more for this very reason, that amid unusual and extraordinary difficulties he both survived himself and preserved the empire.'[11]

From the above pen-picture of Marcus's life, it is clear that his strong personal beliefs supported him through almost two decades of massive leadership responsibilities, multiple bereavements, bitter disappointments and betrayals by those closest to him. They even preserved him from the corruption of virtue that is said inevitably to accompany absolute power: he remained modest, charitable, undaunted and true to his principles to the end.

I hope that Marcus Aurelius, wherever he is, will not be too displeased with my attempt to extract a set of coherent beliefs from notes never intended for this purpose.

Alan Stedall
Birmingham, England, December 24, 2004

1

The Death of an Emperor

H IS BREATH came now raspingly and, although the fever had left him for some hours, his face was ashen and clammy with cold sweat. With what seemed superhuman effort he turned on the narrow field bed and called out to me, 'Rufus, why has night fallen so suddenly?' The evening light, however, continued to filter unchanged almost horizontally through the window of his sparsely furnished bedroom, lighting his bed and the wall against which it stood. The darkness that had fallen on him spoke more of his rapidly weakening condition than that of the northern sun setting outside in a reddish glow.

His son had left him several hours before, despite his father's vain pleading for him to remain until the end, now that this was so imminent. Commodus had been unheeding and had made his departure, his stated concern being that he should not contract his father's disease. Now only his first-line army officers stayed with Marcus to accompany his final hours. It was not that we were unafraid of contracting the pestilence that consumed him, but how could we abandon the man who had led us so selflessly, and given his all in the interests of Rome?

I took his hand, the hand that for the moment still ruled the greatest empire the world had ever known but which was now so weak that it had lost the strength even to grip. He looked at me, his eyes still blue and observant, but with a gaze that seemed to look through me to a world beyond. His voice was barely a whisper and I leant forward to hear him.

'Tell Commodus to lead the Danube legions forward and well. Their loyalty to me has been unswerving and they deserve the best of leaders. Only by moving our armies forward to secure our borders can we hope to pre-serve all that is great and noble that is Rome.' It was clear that his thoughts, now even at the very end, remained focused on his great task: to preserve and defend the empire he had inherited.

He hesitated, closing his eyes for a moment only to open them again. 'And tell the army, if they love me, to protect and safeguard my son.'

This, then, was the father's dying concern, that we should protect his only living son, Commodus. Commodus, who at that very moment was hastening back to Rome in anticipation of his father's death, to claim sole command of the Empire.

I nodded, hoping he could still see me. Then my head sagged and to my embarrassment a lone tear trickled down my right cheek. He saw it and gave a faint smile. 'Weep not for me, think rather of the general pestilence and the deaths that have befallen so many others.' [12] With these characteristic, self-effacing words, he fell silent for the last time. He turned over and covered his head with his bed sheet, as if to sleep, and we left him in peace.

In the morning we found what we grimly expected: the Emperor lay dead. We laid his left hand upon his chest and crossed it with the right, as is customary. We closed his eyes and placed a coin on each to hold the eyelids in place until final rigor mortis had set in, rendering the coins unnecessary.

So died Imperator Caesar Marcus Aurelius Antoninus Augustus, Emperor of the Roman Empire, commander-in-chief of our armies, statesman, sage and philosopher, the greatest and best of all the Roman Emperors. Worn out at the age of fifty-eight, for nineteen long years he had tirelessly held back the barbarians from the furthermost reaches of our Empire, leading our armies to fight them in northern forests and eastern plains and deserts.

More importantly he had ruled the Empire with justice, humility and wisdom. Beloved by all, but especially by his loyal Danubian legions, his loss was to be grieved universally. Now the Empire would pass to Marcus's only surviving son, Commodus. In stark contrast to his father, Commodus was to lead us into confusion, strife and eventual civil war. But this was of course unknown to us at the

time – and anyway this narrative concerns my Lord and
friend, Marcus Aurelius, not his worthless, eventually
insane, son.

I had first met Marcus when I was promoted to Prefect
of the Praetorian Guard twelve years earlier. My background was humble indeed; I was a son and grandson of
soldiers descended from ancient farming stock of Falerii,
north of Rome. I had joined the army twenty years before
and had risen to the rank of Legatus when, in the seventh
year of Marcus's reign, I was promoted first to Prefect
of the City Police of Rome, then to Prefect of Egypt and
finally to Prefect of the Praetorian Guard, the ultimate
military rank – and all within the same year!

However, it must be said that my rapid ascendancy was
only partly a reflection of my qualities as a capable and loyal
soldier. The situation of the Empire was desperate.
Enemies of Rome on our eastern and northern boundaries
threatened both Greece and Italy with invasion. At the
same time a curse had fallen upon the Empire that weakened our capability to defend ourselves as never before.

Under Senator Avidius Cassius, our eastern army had
vanquished the mighty Parthian enemy who had threatened us in Mesopotamia and driven him back beyond the
Tigris River. Unfortunately Cassius had then permitted his
army to sack the friendly Hellenic city of Seleucia, an
ancient city that had opened its gates to him and welcomed
him as liberator. In retribution for Cassius's act, the gods

imposed a deadly curse on his army in that far off province. When Rome welcomed the returning army of Cassius as heroes, they did not see the grim spectres riding alongside each charioteer and marching within the ranks of his legions: harbingers of the plague.

Within weeks of the army's return, thousands of the Romans who had celebrated the victory lay dead in the streets. The numbers of dead were so great that carts and wagons were used to collect this grim cargo. Cemeteries became so crowded that edicts had to be issued to forbid the burying of bodies in graves owned and already occupied by others. In the months that followed, whole farms in nearby provinces became deserted, their fruit rotting on the vines because those who would have harvested it had themselves been plucked from life. This undermined the economy and tax revenues collapsed. The state struggled to find the money it needed to pay its armies and subsidise the friendly states on our borders that were our buffers against barbarian invasion.

The deadly pestilence not only snatched away vast numbers of citizens, farmers and senators, but also slew through the ranks of our legions so that some almost ceased to exist other than in name. No mortal enemy ever inflicted such losses on the military might of Rome. One of the many thousands who fell to the pestilence was Furius Victorinus, Prefect of the Praetorian Guard – hence my urgent appointment as his successor.

This then was the situation that faced me when I rose to the highest military rank Rome had to offer. It fell to me to provide the bodyguard for the Emperor both in Rome and on his field campaigns. The Praetorian Guard was an elite military unit, the final line of defence for the Emperor. Were we to prove unable to protect him, we would be honour bound to fall in battle where we fought, since the Guard chose death before flight or surrender in the protection of the Emperor. It was also my dubious privilege to extend this same protection to the sixteen-year-old Commodus when Marcus made him joint emperor at the outset of his last Danubian campaigns. What a shame we failed to fail in our duty in his respect! Had we allowed a foraging band of barbarians to steal away the young wretch at that time how many good Roman lives would have been saved!

As Praetorian Prefect I had necessarily stayed close to Emperor Marcus, constantly alert for threats to his life. It was during our years of companionship in city, field and strife that I grew to understand and admire him. It is my privilege to commit some of our conversations to paper, as honestly as my memory allows.

2

The Philosopher King

BEFORE I MET Emperor Marcus I heard many stories about him. 'A living philosopher of the first order, a true Stoic,' some said. 'A great general, a strategist, a leader, a real soldier who leads his men from the front and is therefore well beloved by them,' said others. 'A great Roman, true to the principles of honour and justice and the gods of Rome,' said yet others.

But Marcus Aurelius was, in style and actions, strikingly different from earlier emperors, and certainly different from those who were to follow.

I had once been told the story of how Marcus had presided over a set of arena games in which a lion-trainer demonstrated an animal whose nature he had so brutalised that it devoured its victims with spectacular ferocity. The Roman crowd had roared in ecstatic pleasure at the blood-thirsty attacks of the animal and the tortured screams of its victims trapped in the arena below. When the final Christian was torn to pieces the spectators clamoured for the Emperor to reward the trainer for the lion's gory

performance. Marcus, however, had sat silently through-
out. Ignoring the baying mob, he now refused to provide
any such reward for the trainer. Later, asked why he had
resisted the clamour of the populace, he replied simply that
he 'failed to see that the man concerned had done anything
deserving of a reward'. Marcus subsequently decreed that
gladiators fight with blunted swords so that blood was not
spilt for common entertainment.

In stark contrast, it was this same emperor who led our
legions in bold and vigorous campaigns against the
enemies of Rome that crowded on our borders! Here was
indeed a new type of emperor, one who followed his own
precepts, who had the courage to lead our armies from the
front and the even greater courage to deny the carnal
appetites of the infamous Roman mob.

My first meeting with Marcus was in the fine and long-
established settlement of Aquileia on the Adriatic coast.
Here he and his co-Emperor and adopted brother Lucius
planned to counter-attack the Germanic tribes, including
the Marcomanni, the Victuali and the Quadi, who threatened to invade our northern borders along the Danube. I
had travelled north from Rome, having arrived there only
days earlier from Egypt. The roads running north to
Aquileia were of good metal, but they passed through wild
forests and plains drenched with spring rain.

As my chariot entered the city gates, I felt excitement
tinged with trepidation. It was much easier to fall from

high office than to gain it: so many sought to replace you. We drew up outside the military headquarters and I climbed the stone steps, ascending from the sunlit parade ground, noisy with drill practice, into the cool dark offices of the Emperor. I passed sentries of my own Praetorian order who recognised and saluted me, allowing me access to the innermost room of the state apartments.

I found Marcus Aurelius sitting at a table studying a map of the Alps. He was a well-built man, with pronounced handsome features and neatly trimmed beard. His curly hair and beard, once dark, were now streaked with grey. His features reflected the weight of the great responsibilities on his shoulders.

I coughed to make my presence known and he looked up at me, not unkindly. I saluted in return, the steel armour of my right arm ringing on my breastplate. He had large expressive blue eyes that gave the impression of observing rather than pointedly looking at you. His mood seemed to lighten at the sight of me: he cast off the weary expression he had unconsciously held when I first caught sight of him.

'Ah, Rufus, I'm glad to see you. Pour us each a glass of wine and take a seat over here.'

I did as I was bidden and handed the glass of red wine to him. He had gestured me to sit on a bench-seat at right angles to his own. He took a long sip of the wine, rolling it over his tongue to savour it. He once again looked troubled.

'We lost Victorinus a month ago to the pestilence, together with half of the entire Guard. Some of the army legions here have suffered yet worse losses. Even though Stoic philosophy would have it otherwise, it's always a terrible business to lose one's comrades, and even worse when it's not in the heat of battle, furthering the cause of Rome, but simply to disease. But come now, Rufus, tell me more about yourself.'

I told him of my simple, rural upbringing in Falerii, how both my father and grandfather had served as soldiers of Rome, and how I had always aspired to serve the State myself. I described my promotion through the ranks, promotion won not in courts as a politician, but on the battlefield as a hardened soldier. Marcus listened to me intently, now and then giving nods of agreement and encouragement.

Coming to the end of my story, I said how much I looked forward to serving him in my new capacity. I assured him of my unswerving loyalty – to death, if that were demanded of me. Marcus then gazed at me thoughtfully in silence for more than a few seconds.

'All of this I already knew of you Rufus. My agents have spent weeks looking into your background and it is indeed without blemish. You are a loyal soldier of Rome and a great captain of your troops. I would not have agreed to your appointment had it been any less so. But tell me, what sort of man are you?'

I looked at him in puzzlement, at which he smiled.

'My Lord, I am a true soldier of Rome.'

Marcus nodded. 'Yes, I can see that. But tell me, for instance, which gods do you serve and worship?'

I felt my face grow heated, feeling this was some kind of trap. Surely it was obvious I worshipped the city gods of Rome? To do less would be treasonable. Was he seeking a means to be rid of me before I even took office?

'My Lord, I worship the state gods of Rome. Every morning without fail, when in Rome, I attend the Temple of Venus. In the field I worship at the icons of regimental gods our cohort carries with it.'

Marcus was smiling at my embarrassment. 'So, you are not a follower of Mithras, then, or', and here his smile became yet broader, 'a Christian?'

'No, my Lord. Some of my best officers are indeed followers of Mithras – it is a religion well suited to the manly duties of a legionnaire – but none of my regiment is Christian. How could they be? Life in the Roman army is unsuitable for a pacifist, let alone one subversive to the state of Rome. As the Christians themselves say, a man cannot have two masters.'

Simply admitting to be a Christian carried a death sentence, and a dishonourable death at that – being thrown to wild beasts in the arena to be torn to pieces for the entertainment of the crowd. I knew now the Emperor was jesting with me.

He nodded approvingly. 'Fear not, Rufus, I am not trying to trick you into declaring yourself a traitor. I am merely trying to understand the spirit within the inner man that drives you. Such things interest me and, if we are to spend much time together, it would be useful to be able to discuss matters outside of campaign tactics, troop dispositions and logistical problems.'

This was not the conversation I had expected to have with the Emperor. I was still cautious, however: Rome swirled with intrigue; to reveal one's beliefs too nakedly could be to expose oneself to great risks. But Marcus seemed relaxed and genuine, without guile or malevolence. He leaned back with a mischievous twinkle in his eye.

'For instance, Rufus, do you consider the gods as benevolent or malicious?'

'Why, if entreated appropriately, with due ritual and respect, benevolent of course.'

I did not understand where this was leading. He nodded at my answer, the glint still in his eye.

'Yes, benevolent – of course,' he repeated, nodding. 'And would you say they are all-powerful?'

'Yes, my Lord, for that is what makes them gods.'

'And all-knowing?' Marcus watched me intently.

'Yes, being all-powerful, they must be all-knowing.'

Marcus paused for a moment, then continued, 'But would you say, Rufus, that there is great evil in the world?'

'At certain times and places, it is true, there *is* such evil.'

'And does it fall upon the innocent as well as the guilty?'

'Yes, being innocent of sin it seems is no protection against evil.'

Marcus smiled amiably. 'If there is such evil, and it falls upon good and bad alike, how can it be that the gods are benevolent?'

He had me trapped with his logic, but it was not a political trap. I realised it was a trap of the dialectic, beloved of Greek philosophers, and smiled in acknowledgement of the cunning of his approach. He smiled back, openly, in return.

'There you have me, Lord. But are you saying that the gods are not benevolent?'

Marcus hesitated. 'Well, Rufus, there can only be a limited number of logical interpretations of the existence of evil in the world, can't there?'

'Such as, Lord?'

'Ah no, Rufus. That would be too easy. To give you what I think is the answer would do nothing to improve your own powers of reason. Moreover, I am a man like yourself and therefore well capable of being wrong. You must always think for yourself and take nothing for granted. Think through the logical possibilities and we will develop our discussions further another time. Regrettably we must move on to more mundane matters. Tell me about your arrangements for supplying our troops on the forthcoming campaign.'

So I talked Marcus through my proposed arrangements. But I had been taken aback and gratified by our first conversation. I left his offices pleased in the knowledge that our Emperor enjoyed the intellectual tussle of philosophical debate. To him, I was to learn, such discussions, which involved much mental dexterity and wrestling with competing ideas, were every bit as important as the arduous physical exercises and military training that he undertook with his men, despite his poor health.

3

Discussions at Aquileia

IN THE MONTHS that followed, Marcus and Lucius led a party across the Alps to inspect the northern outposts. Marcus had never before left Italy and was awestruck at the magnificence of this mountain range. We stayed at the headquarters of the 14th Legion at Carnuntum on the Danube. The Danube legions were staunch followers of Mithras and both Emperors paid homage not only at the local shrine dedicated to Jupiter but also at the temple of Mithras: to have done any less would have been to invite disaster to the legions stationed there, and so those legions would have interpreted it.

The barbarian tribes to the north were quiet at this time, but Marcus was convinced that they were biding their time, waiting for our army, already weakened by pestilence, to drop its guard on this section of the frontier. Consequently a new command centre was set up and two more legions were raised for the area. With these arrangements in place, we returned once more to winter on the coast at Aquileia.

There we met two celebrated experts, one of the physical world, the other of the metaphysical worlds that lie
beyond, both having been summoned by Marcus, who
aimed to employ the best minds in the civilised world to
end the plague. Galen, a brilliant Hellenic doctor and
philosopher from Pergamon in Mysia, had earned a world-
wide reputation in the practical study of medicine and
anatomy. Harnouphis was a celebrated Egyptian priest
and renowned sorcerer, a high priest of the Egyptian god
Isis. One of his first actions was to dedicate an altar at
Aquileia to Isis as protector of the populace and legion.
Thus Marcus had invoked both science and religion to rid
us of the pestilence.

On several evenings at Aquileia I had the privilege of
joining the two Emperors, Marcus and Lucius, at private
meals held with Galen and Harnouphis. As Prefect of the
Guard I tended merely to observe rather than actively
participate in the discussions at table, though I knew
Marcus would not have objected to my so doing.

The occasion of the first meal was not best for conversation. This was not due to any deficiency in the food or
wine, both of which were plentiful and of good quality, but
because of the diverse nature of the participants. Marcus
was, of his nature, quiet and considered but amiable. He
had eaten sparsely and drunk little, possibly because of his
chronic stomach condition, of which, however, he never
complained. Lucius in contrast had eaten great quantities

of flesh, washed down by an equally large quantity of wine, which he drank but seemed not to savour.

Lucius had dominated the early part of the conversation, describing the many jesters, actors, jugglers, harpists, flautists and mime actors he had brought back with him from his recent expedition to Syria and Alexandria. As the wine flowed, Lucius became ever more effusive in describing the many attractive features and details of each entertainer, expressing regret that he had been unable to bring them to Aquileia and saying how impatiently he longed to return to Rome to rejoin them. Lucius seemed unaware or unconcerned that his long colourful description of his troupe had elicited at best only a polite acknowledgement from those around the table. Indeed, his conversation had become a monologue, with little involvement from others in the party, though Harnouphis smiled and nodded at appropriate points.

Harnouphis had a shaven head and finely cut, aesthetic features, enhanced by carefully applied cosmetics, as is customary for Egyptian priests. His dress was oriental in style, uninfluenced by Roman standards. He had picked at his meal and drunk only a little spring water. His bird-like features now showed he was following the conversation attentively, but seemingly more in an attempt to understand the speakers and gauge their characters rather than from any real interest in the topic. When he did participate in the conversation it was with obvious care, watching the reaction of those addressed and crafting his words to their pleasure. His statements seemed often to be deliberately enigmatic, perhaps to emphasise the mystical nature of his sorcerer's craft, perhaps merely to avoid stating a view so clearly that it could elicit opposition from others at the table.

The behaviour of Galen was also in marked contrast to that of his fellows. Dark and bearded, as was typical of Hellenic philosophers, he bore his world-renowned intellect with only a half-hidden haughtiness. He had eaten fastidiously, using his knife on the served meats with precision, as if still at Pergamon dissecting one of the defeated gladiators from whom he gained so much anatomical knowledge. As Lucius waxed ever more voluble and effusive in praise of his Middle Eastern entertainers, so Galen's part in the conversation diminished and his impatience with such triviality increased. It was my impression that, had it not been for his genuine respect and affection for Marcus, he would have excused himself from the table, feigning a headache or similar.

Marcus had been quietly observing his guests for some time, amiably allowing his young adopted brother to monopolise the conversation. However, it seemed he now recognised the need to intervene, if only to preserve Galen's good humour. He leant forward and placed a hand on Lucius's shoulder.

'Be patient a little longer, Lucius, we will soon have you

back in Rome and there you can once more enjoy the entertainment of the gifted artists you brought from Alexandria. However, I would like to change the conversation entirely. I am anxious to take the benefit of the wisdom of our two celebrated guests. It is seldom that one is at a table with two persons who between them command the complete span of understanding of both the physical and metaphysical worlds.'

Lucius fell into a reluctant silence, indicating irritably to the serving maid that his wine glass be replenished. Harnouphis smiled unctuously at Marcus's warm praise: if he had been a cat he would by now have been purring. Galen seemed to have been called back from whatever distant Mysian plain he had removed himself and nodded his encouragement to Marcus: 'Lord, I am here to render you such service and advice as my scientific learning allows.'

Marcus graciously returned Galen's nod and sat back to compose his thoughts and words carefully. 'Would you say, my friends, that it better to have a short life or better to have a long life?'

4

On the Brevity of Life
and the Need to Seek Meaning

I RECOGNISED from Marcus's words and expression his intention of having a little intellectual sport with his guests.

Lucius was the first to answer, without hesitation or consideration. He placed his glass down momentarily. 'That's a simple enough question, Marcus. There is a common saying, "A short life but a merry one", also "Eat, drink and be merry, for tomorrow you die."' He sat back and belched, evidently satisfied to have dismissed the question at a stroke.

'Thank you, brother,' Marcus nodded at Lucius, smiling. He turned to the Hellenic physician. 'Do you agree with him, Doctor Galen?'

Galen considered his half-empty wine glass and was silent for more than a few seconds. Only then, looking up at Marcus, did he speak. 'I would say, Lord, that a life should be long enough for the gaining of wisdom, but not so long that the soul finds itself entombed in the decrepitude of a fast-degenerating body. Once the pains and discomforts of old age weigh heavily upon us, it is surely time for us to be gone.'

Again, Marcus nodded amiably at Galen's words, then he turned to the Egyptian priest and sorcerer. 'And what is your thinking, esteemed Harnouphis?'

Harnouphis also took some time to consider the question, carefully looking around the table so as to tailor his words to best effect. 'I would say that it is not for us to judge whether it is better to lead a short or a long life. The destiny of each individual is foretold in the stars, celestial bodies which were set in the heavens by the gods at the outset of creation. Therefore the gods have already fore-ordained the span of earthly existence of each of us, and what the gods have determined is not for us to challenge, be it a short life or a long life.'

Harnouphis scanned the faces round the table and was pleased to find that his words seemed to have found general acceptance. At least they had not aroused fierce opposition.

Marcus nodded encouragingly to Harnouphis, but it was obvious from his bearing that he was not going to let the matter rest there. 'Wise words from each of you, friends. But surely, Lucius, a short life that is merry but ill-considered, is a life less than noble, and, according to the great Socrates, one not worth living?'

Lucius's expression showed him to be less than happy at his opinion being subjected to criticism, no matter how gentle, in front of guests. He turned to Marcus with more than a slight display of petulance: 'That may well be what Socrates said, my dear Marcus, but then Socrates spent his whole life debating the meaning of life in the streets of Athens, and what good did it do for Athens? Did such discussions strengthen their armies against their foes, or enable them to fill their granaries with more grain? And what good did it do Socrates? The only thanks he received from his fellow Athenians was a cup of hemlock! It seems to me that to seek too profoundly for the meaning and purpose of life is to waste the brief time the gods have granted to us here on this earth.'

Marcus listened to his brother's challenge without any display of irritation, even though it was apparent to all present that Lucius was belittling Marcus's renowned pursuit of philosophy.

When Marcus spoke, it was in a slow, calm voice: 'My dear Lucius, while it is of the essential nature of all animals to be conscious, as far as we are aware it is only man that is self-conscious. This ability to detach his thinking sufficiently to contemplate himself and his own existence and that of others is, as far as we know, unique to our species.

'This leads directly to a position that fundamentally distinguishes man from the rest of the animal kingdom: his awareness of the transient nature of his own existence. To quote an unknown poet: "We wait a billion years to be born to a life that is, against the backdrop of eternity, as brief as the flicker of a shooting star."

'As far as we are aware, no other animal has this perspective on its life, gained by sufficient self-conscious capacity to contemplate its own inevitable personal demise. Consciousness beyond our present physical existence is unimaginable for most of us and may well, indeed, be a contradiction in terms. In any event, it may be an irresolvable limitation of our essentially animal mind to contemplate our continued existence in non-animal terms.'

Marcus looked around at his guests, slightly embarrassed at leading the conversation so forthrightly. Then he continued in the same moderate tones: 'This unique nature and perspective of mankind is a major influencer of our individual lives. Faced with the inevitability of our own individual mortality, we each find it necessary to conjure up some strategy to accommodate what is, for most us, the naked prospect of a fearful and dreaded journey from awareness into the unknown from whence we came.

'In the face of eventual mortality, fully effective life-strategies for an individual to pursue would be, in the first instance, to seek to extend his life indefinitely and, in the second instance, to establish the form of landscape that lies beyond his mortal existence.

'Regarding the first instance, while medical science, thanks to the brilliant efforts of Doctor Galen here, has achieved significant progress in relative terms in extending human existence, in absolute cosmic terms its progress is, of course, infinitesimal.

'Regarding the second instance, with due respect to the esteemed Harnouphis,' and here Marcus graciously nodded to the high priest of Isis, 'there is no single view of a life after death that is universally held.

'Hence, given our present limited progress in pursuit of the two most effective strategies, the individual is forced back on lesser strategies that patently fail to confront and address the fundamental issue involved. These must, in consequence, be regarded as arguably merely palliative.'

Marcus paused to take a sip of wine before continuing. 'The most common strategy adopted is the one, my dear Lucius, that you espouse: to attempt to revert back to a blissful state of denial and feign the same ignorance of our fate as our less "gifted" fellow animal creatures.'

Lucius looked a little troubled at this remark. Marcus nodded kindly to him and continued: 'Essentially this strategy is best defined as you have succinctly put it, dear Lucius, "The purpose of life is to be happy and not dwell too much on its brevity." And I agree with you that, for most people, this strategy is sufficient to see them through, along the lines of "Eat, drink and be merry, for tomorrow you die."

'Certainly as a life-strategy it has much to recommend it: it is easy to adopt; it is not too intellectually demanding. Also, unless pursued to extremes, it does not throw you into conflict with your fellow man and it supports unburdened behaviours and a positive frame of mind. Indeed, there are very few disadvantages to this strategy, which is why it is so popular and widely held, if only in a non-reflective manner.

'However, in adopting this life-strategy the individual is required to fill his life with sufficient distracting activity to prevent the unpleasant and non-accommodated reality of his own mortality intruding upon his thoughts and emotions. Lack of sufficient activity results in depression, which, due to its antisocial characteristics, can be self-reinforcing. A further disadvantage to this strategy is that, if unwillingly thrust into a conscious "endgame" of existence, the individual might find himself finally faced with a last journey for which he is both unprepared and unwilling to make. However, arguably, in overall terms, this is perhaps a small price to pay for what is, in effect, a brief non-reflective sojourn in this thing called conscious life.'

Marcus again sipped his wine, then resumed. The others listened intently to his words. 'However, for some tenacious individuals, a path of deliberate denial on such fundamental matters is both intellectually insufficient and offensive. They argue that a deliberate decision to avoid coming to an intellectual accommodation with their own inevitable mortality is no kind of accommodation, or at the very least a wholly unsatisfactory accommodation.

'To quote Socrates again: for some, at least, "an unreflective life is not worth living". Why do some people, including myself, and Doctor Galen here, hunger to understand and find a rational meaning to life?'

Here, Marcus turned to his fellow philosopher for a contribution to the discussion, but Galen declined, encouraging Marcus to continue: 'Lord, please proceed to share your thinking with us.'

Marcus resumed, but with what seemed like continuing reluctance: 'Arguably, the fundamental requirement of the animal mind, including that of man, is to make sense of what is perceived. Without this ability the animal would be immersed in an ever-changing and senseless chaos of light, sound and physical experiences. As a consequence of being unable to interpret, and hence unable to interact with, the outside world, such an animal must perish.

'It is therefore vital that some form of mental interpretation be imposed on the animal's perceptions. This includes an understanding of the concept of "time" that can link a series of "frames" of perception into a logical order and consequently allow explanations of events. Also, the formation of mental models of what the material world is, and how it interacts with itself and with the animal.

'Beyond the fundamental requirement of animals to understand reality is a further requirement for them to be able to interact with and influence reality positively and predictably by making use of the understanding they have gained. An animal that understood the world but was unable to use this knowledge in a practical way would not be able to sustain itself.

'The requirement to be able to interpret reality, for the purpose of being able to interact with it and so transform it into a future aspired state, is so fundamental to a living organism that it has given rise to that function within the animal that we term "intelligence".'

Harnouphis here interjected, 'Surely much under-standing and knowledge is gained without any pre-defined intent to put it to use – that is to say, it is gained in simple idle curiosity, or in pursuit of the theoretical sciences?'

Marcus nodded and replied, 'I would agree, but the counter-argument here is that such knowledge, once gained, cannot but influence future behaviour, unless we deliberately choose to ignore it – which, of course, would be extremely difficult. Increasing the richness of the tapes-try of one's understanding must inevitably increase the comfort (or discomfort) of our awareness of the material world. Knowledge, therefore, is not only power but, of its nature, it modifies actions and behaviour.

'It is therefore predictable that an intelligent animal will, of its essential nature, resolutely impose a satisfactory meaning on life, and seek to transform reality for its own benefit. For what else is any animal's purpose in understanding the world?'

Marcus looked around him to ensure that he held the interest of those present. With the possible exception of Lucius, it was apparent that he did. He went on: 'At first consideration it would seem that the more accurate and rich the map of reality the intellectual capacity of an animal is capable of sustaining, the more effective it will be in interacting with the world, and hence the greater its chances of survival.

'In an environment that is sufficiently benevolent to reward rational behaviour, it would seem logical that the gods would create animals that are increasingly intelligent and thus increasingly effective in mapping the scope, content and detail of the reality in which they find themselves. The improved richness of their mental map of the universe must surely give them an advantage? On what other basis could we explain the rise to supremacy of man?

'But suppose the animal advances to a point where it actually begins to comprehend the transient nature of its own existence? Through its own inherent coercion to understand, it would be forced to confront, and attempt to comprehend, a fundamentally incomprehensible landscape (if any) of what lies beyond its own brief existence. Such a challenge, once engaged, would at the very least be unsettling, and at worst it could lead to depression and insanity.

'Uncertain, depressed or insane animals will not lead favoured existence. So we should not be surprised that natural selection in the human species tends to weed out individuals with such disadvantageous characteristics, favouring those individuals *and peoples* with innate natural strategies that avoid such unhelpful behaviour. Furthermore, we might well expect to find that natural selection evolves effective strategies, including the capping of intelligence, to ensure that the individual is not driven by an intellectual need to accommodate what it is incapable of comprehending.

'It may also be that, *through social evolution*, the fundamental animal drive to understanding is restricted by social mechanisms – for example, social structures that hand responsibility for understanding the metaphysical nature of things to appointed priests, or even to some external, deliberately incomprehensible, Supreme Being. The latter strategy would be particularly attractive: the unfathomable nature of what lies beyond our earthly existence may thus be cloaked by an equally incomprehensible, but *perceived to be communicable*, Supreme Being. This provides a comforting, rational, quasi-human interface along otherwise highly uncomfortable boundaries between our existence and the infinite, which we are driven to try to understand.

'However, one could argue that religion – any religion – is not an imposition of understanding upon reality but a conscious and willing *surrender of any attempt at understanding ultimate reality* in the face of the impossibility of the task – "a surrender of reason to faith".

'Each of these naturally selected or socially evolved, strategies offers the individual a buffer against a potentially catastrophic conflict between man's fundamental drive to understand on the one hand and the essentially incomprehensible nature of reality on the other. He thus avoids a collision between the irresistible force of the sentient being's need to impose meaning and the immovable object of the incomprehensibility of non-sentient existence.'

Marcus stopped and looked around the table for a response. Clearly much of what he had said had been entirely lost on Lucius. It was Harnouphis who spoke first, as if unwillingly, his voice tremulous at the possible impertinence of what he was about to say: 'Are you saying, Lord, that you believe that there is no life after death and that the gods are simply a social construct to avoid facing this unpleasant fact?'

Marcus was unperturbed and, smiling, took a sip from his glass. As he continued his gaze remained fixed on the glass in his hand: 'My dear Harnouphis, I am not saying that – no man can be certain of such things. I merely set out a line of reasoning to you that might suggest such a thing is possible. I for my part am convinced that gods do exist. We see them fixed in the firmament at night for all to observe.'

Marcus then looked up at his guests. 'What I am saying is that to flinch from an attempt to establish a good purpose for my life, and meaning for the universe in which I find myself, is for me no more acceptable than to lay down arms in the middle of battle. And the arms that we each possess in our battle for such understanding are reason and philosophy.'

Lucius appeared thoroughly bored at Marcus's explanation of why, for him at least, a philosophical engagement with life was so vital.

Marcus turned now to Galen. 'But let us go back to the original question. Is it better to have a short life or a long one?

'Esteemed doctor, your words were well considered, but there are those who choose to end their lives early, before the onset of old age, either by their own hands or by deliberately placing themselves at certain risk of death for the sake of their cause. Many legionnaires have sacrificed themselves on the field of battle for the sake of their comrades and for the glory of Rome. Christians also willingly go to their deaths, although they of course are trained to do so and die singing in the arena because they believe that by dying such a death they pass to eternal life. So it is clear that not all men choose to cling to life until driven from it by the extreme pains of old age, as you suggest.

'Harnouphis, you amongst us know most about the worlds beyond this earthly realm and the intentions of the gods. However, while the gods foreordain our fates, they also give us intellect and free will. It follows that they require us to use these gifts – not to challenge their will but to interpret it, to pursue it to the best of our ability. They also accord us choice in how to live our lives. This will in part dictate the span of our existence. The life of a Roman legionary is likely to be more glorious but much shorter than the life of a common herdsman.'

Marcus still held the attention of Galen and Harnouphis, but Lucius appeared to be inebriated to the point of nodding off. Marcus continued, however. 'Harnouphis, tell me, is it possible for a man to lose more than he possesses?'

Harnouphis looked perplexed at the apparent simplicity of such a question. 'No, Lord. By definition a man must first possess an item for it to be taken away from him.'

'Agreed, Harnouphis. And would you say that at any moment we possess our future?'

'Not at any instant. Our future is yet to come: we cannot possess it until it becomes the present.'

'And what of the past? Can we possess the past?'

'The past is but a recollection, a record. We may accrue present honour or ignominy from it, but the past itself we cannot possess.'

Marcus nodded. 'So the only part of our lives we really possess is the present?'

'Yes. At any instant in our life we possess only that moment.'

'So, given that all men possess only the present, their loss of it upon death must be equal, whether they have lived long lives or short?'

Harnouphis and Galen both nodded their acceptance of such logic. Lucius appeared lost in sleepy thought – perhaps he was already back in Rome with his troupe.

5

On the Pursuit of Purpose

GALEN DRANK from his glass and beckoned for it to be filled. 'That may be so, Lord: I see that one can argue that it does not matter whether we have long or short lives as all we lose on death is the present moment. But that is not to say that a life can be valued simply by its duration.'

Marcus looked interested. 'If not by duration, then how else would you say that one man's life is more valuable than another's? Surely, if all any man possesses is that very instant at which he is living, then the loss of it must be as significant to him as to any other man?'

'Yes, *to him* – but that is an entirely subjective point of view. To assess the relative value of any two things we need common, objective criteria.'

Marcus was thoughtful for a few long moments as if refining his own ideas on this point Galen had raised. *Is it possible to say that one man's life is inherently more valuable than another's? If not, how could anyone choose one way of life as being superior to another?*

Marcus settled himself in his seat. 'Doctor Galen, I understand that you are convinced that each and every element of the body has its own specific function. Am I correct in this understanding of your teaching?'

Galen looked uncertain as to the direction the conversation was now taking but nonetheless replied, 'You have correctly grasped the principles I have established, Lord. The human body has been so designed by the gods that each of its component parts has a particular purpose and cannot be improved upon.'

Marcus nodded. 'So, can you conceive that any part of the body could exist without purpose? Is there a part that adds nothing to the general well-being of the body as a whole?'

'No, that would be against logic, science and the will of the gods. Such a body part, although superfluous to the whole, would continue to take of its share of the body's vitality. In doing so, not only would it fail to add to the general well-being of the body, but it would actually, in small or major part, drain the body of some of its vitality. It would be parasitic in nature. The body does not naturally act as a host to parasitic elements.'

Marcus nodded his understanding. 'So, each component of the body has been created, by nature and the gods, to have a particular purpose that contributes to the greater well-being of the whole. Surely such a natural law must continue to apply at the next level of nature's hierarchy?

Each man must have a purpose in society, a purpose that contributes to the greater good of the state which protects and nourishes him?'

Galen looked thoughtful. 'That would be a logical extension of my teaching. Without such a purpose an individual would at best be a drone in the hive, consuming a portion of the hive's treasure but contributing nothing – he would be a social parasite or, worse, a criminal.'

Marcus looked gratified at the direction the conversation was taking under his guidance. 'So, friends, I think we are agreed that, for a person to be a worthwhile member of society, he or she must have a contribution to make to it. It follows that a life led without social purpose is, from the perspective of one's fellow man, worthless.

'Clearly it is possible to lead a hedonistic life of self-indulgence, but this is of value to society only so long as one has gold in one's purse to pay for such a lifestyle. Beyond its value to the keepers of inns and brothels, such a life has no intrinsic merit for society.'

The volume of wine imbibed by Lucius was finally having a completely soporific effect. He lay back in his seat, his mouth open and his eyes closed, insensible to any umbrage he might otherwise have taken at Marcus's words.

Marcus continued, 'It follows that a worthwhile life must have purpose. And from the perspective of society, this must be a purpose that benefits one's fellow man. Furthermore, to have a purpose a life must also be *considered*: without consideration one is unlikely to live purposefully other than by happy chance.'

Galen nodded in agreement. 'So the value of a man's life can be measured in terms of his contribution to society? That would seem both logical and reasonable.'

But Harnouphis intervened: 'But where is the objective measure of the individual's contribution? What measure indicates that the contribution of a senator is greater than that of a road-sweeper? They both do service to the state. Both may be conscientious, each to the best of his ability.'

Galen picked up the point. 'The measure must be a combination of the scale of their contribution to society and the scarcity of the skills needed to deliver it. A poorly performing road-sweeper would leave a few city streets dirty; a poorly performing senator could lose Rome one of its provinces. Also, most men could, if they so chose, sweep a road; few, however, have the intellect and powers of oratory to be a senator of Rome. This is the common rule of the marketplace: when the supply of a commodity is scarce, the price placed upon it by those who wish to possess it increases.'

Harnouphis hesitated before he nodded. 'I can see that – and also that, from the point of view of society, an individual life should contribute to the well-being of the community which secures his existence. But it does not necessarily follow that, from the perspective of the individual, such a purpose in life is best for him. The best that can be said is that, by living a socially responsible life, he conforms to the moral constructs imposed by society and that this is likely to win him approval.'

Marcus nodded. 'Yes, if one takes the position that a moral sense of duty to society is simply a social construct, of no innate ethical value to the individual, then such a challenge would be rational. But I would argue that one of man's distinguishing characteristics is that he is, above all, a social animal. It is not possible for him to live a civilised life on his own, without the support of his fellow men. Indeed, it could be argued that a civilised life apart from society is a contradiction in terms. If you accept this then you must surely accept that to live a life that contributes nothing to society is contrary to the essential nature of man.'

Galen intervened: 'But what if an individual were to accept that his actions were unnatural to his species but yet persist in them? All societies have their robbers and villains. No doubt they would accept that their way of life is unsociable, but they care not a jot about it. Indeed, they would probably argue that, while their way of life may be unnatural to society, it is this very difference that they depend on. It allows them the opportunity to predate upon law-abiding citizens. They might also argue that such a lifestyle, while unnatural to society, is very natural to them and their criminal associates. How would you convince them of the error of their thinking?'

Marcus was unmoved. 'We have already established that a key characteristic of man is his advanced level of intellect. This not only renders him self-conscious but also grants him awareness of the condition of his fellow men – it gives him empathy. If an individual persists in actions that inflict suffering or deprivation upon other people, we must conclude that either he is ignorant of the consequences of his actions or that, while he has such understanding, he is indifferent to the effect of his actions. If we show him the damage that he does to others and he persists in his criminal activity, we are then forced to conclude that he lacks the fellow feeling that is an essential characteristic of a civilised human being. We may not blame him for his flawed nature, which is not of his own making, but we are beholden to take such action as is necessary to protect society from his malicious behaviour.'

Galen considered Marcus's reply. 'So you consider that an individual who does not recognise that his purpose in life is to add value to society and thus is either idle or disruptive, fails to qualify as a citizen of that society and therefore falls outside the bounds of our discussion?'

Marcus nodded. 'Succinctly put, Doctor Galen. However, I would offer you an additional argument point: a person is happiest when he has the best opportunity of using his natural talents. Would you not agree with me?'

Galen assented. 'Certainly it is difficult to visualise how an individual could be happy if he were prevented from exercising his god-given talents. Indeed it is only in this way that he is likely to make his way in the world.'

Marcus drained his cup. 'Then I would conclude that the best purpose of an individual's life is to find the vehicle for his natural talents that most benefits society. And since the best way of using his talents is the one which is most natural, that is the one that is most likely to bring him satisfaction.'

6

On the Supreme Good

GALEN LISTENED carefully while Marcus summed up, then opened a new topic of conversation. 'Lord, we can agree that the best choice for an individual is to seek a means of using his god-given talents for the benefit of society, but what would you say is the supreme good in life? What should a man seek to possess above all else?'

Without waiting for a response from the others around the table, Galen continued somewhat pompously to answer his own question, as if it had been rhetorical: 'I for my part would say that a man's most precious possession is his health. Good health is fundamental to all his activities in this world. If a man's health fails him that puts an end to all his endeavours.'

Marcus turned encouragingly to Harnouphis, who took a moment's thought before responding: 'I would say that his most precious possession is the love and esteem in which he is held by the gods. It is they who dictate his fate, his good fortune and his health. Woe to him who incurs the disfavour of the gods.'

Marcus nodded at these words. 'But ultimately, my friends, a man's health or good fortune must desert him. He will die either on the battlefield or in his bed. Is a man then inevitably destined to lose his most precious possession?'

Galen responded: 'As all men are born to die, they must of course lose their lives through either ill-fortune or failing health. And is life not their most precious possession?'

Marcus did not hesitate in his reply: 'For some men, who cling to life beyond all reason and honour, yes. But others, it seems to me, freely give up their lives for causes they believe in. For them life itself was not their most precious possession.

'We are each ultimately destined to lose the material things we possess: good fortune, health, fame, wealth – and life itself. We even lose our loved ones, when they are taken from us, or we from them. If we place the greatest value upon such things then we are destined for grief and despair. There is, however, one further blessing in life which no loss of health or fortune, no man or even god can take from us once we have wholly won it. Not even death can rob us of it.'

Galen spoke: 'I accept that we must all lose wealth, health and pleasure on our deaths, but surely, of those things you mention, true fame can prove enduring? We continue to do honour to those who have passed before us in exemplary and heroic lives. Consider Augustus and Trajan. They remain heroes of the state of Rome to this day.'

Marcus nodded. 'Yes, they remain heroes to Rome, and it is right that we continue to honour them, but do they now know of it? And how could they have been certain of it at the time? It is no more logical to strive for the adulation of generations yet unborn than it is to grumble that our forefathers do not pay us the respect we feel is due from them. The spirits of the heroes you name have returned from whence they came. It is unlikely that their ashes take much comfort from the adulation they now receive.'

Galen and Harnouphis both looked perplexed. It was Harnouphis who spoke first: 'Then, pray tell us, Lord, what is this ultimate possession imperishable even in death?'

Marcus hesitated before speaking. 'My friends, it is peace of mind. It is the soul content with itself. It is the spirit at rest. Once this treasure is our complete possession, no loss of fortune, wealth or health can trouble us. Death itself will not disturb us: we will see it as the false menace it is.'

Galen and Harnouphis fell silent for some minutes as they considered Marcus's words. Harnouphis eventually spoke: 'Clearly if a man can win for himself an untroubled mind then, by definition, nothing can further trouble him. But is this not a tautology that fails to move the argument forward? Does it not re-state the same truth in different words?'

Marcus responded: 'If we left the subject there, then of course you would be right. We would simply be observing that the only basis of ultimate contentment is an untroubled mind, and this does indeed seem like tautology. But consider further. If we agree this statement, we rule out other imagined routes to happiness such as the pursuit of pleasure, wealth, fame or health because we recognise that we must ultimately lose each of these, and with their loss goes such temporary and transient happiness they might have brought us.'

There was again a long silence that seemed to last several minutes, and which was eventually broken by Harnouphis: 'How then are we to win for ourselves a peace of mind that can never be taken from us?'

Marcus paused before replying: 'There is more than one road, and more than one philosophy that purports to offer such peace of mind. One can withdraw from life, either physically or spiritually – perhaps both. If one chooses not to value anything in life, it follows that one cannot then be deprived of anything of value. Such, broadly, were the teachings of Diogenes, who held most material things in contempt and doubted that true sincerity or integrity could be found in men. There is clearly an underlying rationality to such a philosophy: if nothing is valued, one does not risk losing anything of value.

'However, it seems to me that this philosophy promotes an unbecoming lack of engagement with life, a general retreat from life. Indeed, such a philosophy would perhaps hold it best not to be born in the first place.

'I am firmly of the view that, since the gods have chosen to place us in the world as creatures of intellect, capable of exercising reason, we are beholden to engage with life, using these talents the gods have granted us. Such engagement places us at risk of disappointment in our endeavours, and grief at our loss of persons and things we love, but this is the price we pay for being born with natural gifts and accompanying obligations.'

Galen was puzzled: 'How then, if we are duty-bound to place ourselves at risk of disappointment, can we achieve that peace of mind you say is our only permanent possession in life?'

Marcus did not respond directly. 'There is, I believe, a way of life that does not flinch from involvement but is yet capable of delivering ultimate peace of mind, regardless of the misfortunes that beset a life of engagement. Consider the possibilities yourself.'

The others fell silent, considering Marcus's challenge. It was Harnouphis who spoke first: 'Lord, in my faith we are convinced a life awaits us after death. We are told that this temporal world is but a shadow of the life to come and that, if we live according to the commandments of our gods, we will pass across the vast voids of time and space into the hereafter. In those eternal worlds we will receive the rewards we have earned through our faithfulness, and our sacrifices and trials in this world.

'It was this belief that encouraged the great Pharaohs to have vast tombs built for them, to protect their earthly bodies as they await the call of our gods that will awaken them into eternal life. Such tombs are equipped with all the earthly possessions and servants that they will need in their lives hereafter.

'Our faith in these matters gives us the peace of mind of which you speak. The fate of our eternal souls is in our own hands. No man can take this from us.'

Another long silence was at last broken by Galen: 'Harnouphis, I envy you your peace of mind based upon the firm convictions you hold. For my part, as a man of science, I have certain practical doubts as to the certainty of a conscious life after death. Why should we believe that our intellect can survive the physical dissolution of our brain? Why have we never received a response from those who have passed over? Where is the accommodation to be found for the multitude of souls of the dead, let alone of those who are yet to die? Our one certainty is that we have no recollection of a life before our birth. We emerge from oblivion. Why, then, should we believe otherwise than that we pass back into oblivion?'

From the rapid colouration of Harnouphis's face I judged he took considerable offence at Galen's challenge to his faith. He tried to interrupt Galen but Marcus gestured kindly to him to hold back: 'Esteemed Harnouphis, this is a dialectical debate. Do not take offence at Doctor Galen's words. If you can see a lack of logic in them, however, then you owe it to those present to point it out.'

However, Harnouphis would not be deflected. 'Lord, I find fault with Galen's words, not on the basis of logic but because his views challenge the temple scriptures of our people. These holy scriptures clearly guarantee an afterlife to all who love and revere the gods. Since they represent the words of our gods, they must be accepted as portraying absolute truth. And the scriptures themselves state that, "He who contradicts these holy scriptures commits blasphemy and thereby risks the wrath of the great ones and all those true believers who revere them." '

Galen and Marcus were taken aback at Harnouphis's untypical firmness of position. Clearly Galen's words had struck a very raw nerve in him. After a pause it was Marcus who spoke first. 'Esteemed Harnouphis, clearly your people hold their temple scriptures dear, but tell me, did your gods write these scriptures directly themselves?'

Harnouphis struggled to regain composure. 'No, Lord, they did not. How could they? They made their wishes known to the ancient prophets, who committed them as words to tablets and scripture.'

'I understand Harnouphis. But tell me, has the man yet been born who is perfect and incapable of error?'

Harnouphis was clearly perplexed at Marcus's question. 'No, Lord, it is in the essential nature of man that he is imperfect; only the gods themselves are without flaw.'

Marcus nodded. 'So, even those who committed to the written word that which they took to be the wishes of the gods were, of their nature, imperfect?'

Harnouphis saw the direction Marcus was taking, and that he was cornered. 'Yes, Lord, even the ancient prophets were men and, as men, shared our imperfect nature.'

'Then, Harnouphis, you must surely agree that, as these scriptures were created by those who, try as they might, were themselves inevitably imperfect, we cannot be certain that they portray the wishes of the gods without flaw.'

Marcus continued, his voice calm and level: 'Clearly it is the right of any individual to choose what scriptures, if any, he regards as holy. But when a man judges another because the other man challenges the words he holds as holy, such judgement rests on foundations that must be suspect, no matter how sincere his faith. It is a rash man indeed who rushes to violent judgement of another on evidence that he must admit is potentially flawed. Any work of man, even if revered as holy, may not be without error. To condemn another, perhaps do him violence, on such beliefs is both unreasonable and cruel.'

Harnouphis fell silent, unable to fault Marcus's words, yet equally unable to accept his conclusion.

Galen continued: 'I repeat that I envy Harnouphis the

peace of mind his faith grants him. I would do nothing to rob him of this. Our spirits may well return, on our death in this world, to the World-Fire from whence they came, but there is at least as much evidence against a conscious life in the hereafter as there is for it. Hence there are many, like myself, of a scientific mind, who are unwilling or unable to surrender our reason to blind faith, despite the peace of mind that such surrender may offer.

'Lord, I am convinced by your argument that our most precious possession is peace of mind, but I reject the paths we have already discussed that offer this – that is, through the denial of this world or by unsubstantiated promises of a world to come. So how else are we to gain the peace of mind of which you speak?'

After a moment Marcus replied: 'Let me more closely grapple with your question: how are we to obtain peace of mind if not by detaching ourselves from this world or attaching ourselves to a world yet to come, having rejected the first case as being unworthy of us and the second as being unreliable? The answer for me is two-fold.

'Firstly, we need to recognise that we do not experience the world directly. The interactions with this world that we experience, we experience only as perceptions through our senses. Such perceptions are then subjected to the judgement of our intellect. It is our intellect that imposes the judgements "good" or "bad" upon our perceptions, and it is our intellect that accordingly flags material objects as desirable or best avoided. In the natural world itself, however, nothing is either good nor bad. It is innocent of the moral judgements we choose to impose upon it.

'Events disturb our peace of mind only because we permit our intellect to allow them to do so. We give our intellect free rein to conspire with our perceptions to disturb us.

'To achieve peace of mind we must discipline our intellect so that it suspends judgement on our perception of those matters over which we have no control. Allow me to give you an example. If a man commits an offence against me and I choose to condemn him for it, then in making this choice I also choose to trouble myself with his sin against me, and with the need to seek retribution. On the other hand, I could accept that, given the nature of this man or his flawed thinking, nothing better could have been expected of him in the first place. I then see that the error was my own in allowing him the opportunity to offend me. My thoughts are then turned from, how to seek retribution against him for his offence, to how I can improve this man by demonstrating to him the error of his ways, thereby turning him from further offence.

'A further example. A man desires a certain woman and prays to his gods that he may possess her. Then he realises how much better it would be if he were to pray that they curtail his lust. He then further realises that this desire is within himself, under his own control, and so he prays to his gods to help him in his pursuit of self-discipline. Finally he understands that such self-discipline is wholly under his own control. He has no need to trouble the gods. He is well able to achieve it through his own efforts. He reminds himself that the man who surrenders himself to his animal passions takes a beast for his master.

'Only through persistent rational control of our responses to the world, through hesitating to impose moral judgements on people, events and things outside our control, and through the healthy discipline of our desires, can we hope to promote our *own best nature* and deliver ourselves the peace of mind that we seek.'

Galen intervened: 'That is more easily said than done, Lord. How many of us can exert the self-control that such a route to peace of mind demands?'

Marcus nodded. 'I accept that it is difficult. But I did say that my answer was two-fold. We have a further source of peace of mind from which to draw strength. Having first recognised the natural attributes of intellect and reason that the gods have granted us, it is from the satisfaction we then gain from deploying these in pursuit of a noble purpose in life. If we are satisfied that we have fulfilled our duty in this regard to the very best of our ability, as a soldier does when he serves his turn in battle, then we can justly claim as our reward the peace of mind that follows.

'To seek the praise of other men, or expect reward in this world or the next for pursuing a life true to our best nature is superfluous to our needs. It actually debases our actions. It alleges that our actions flow from a desire for material advantage rather than the pure desire to conform to our own true potential.

'The peace of mind that flows from our pursuit of virtue and duty, be it ultimately successful or unsuccessful, is more than sufficient reward for our actions. We need no other acknowledgement.'

Galen and Harnouphis exchanged glances as if wondering who was to speak first. It was Galen who said, 'Lord, this is a hard path, indeed, to the peace of mind we seek. It demands that we be critical not only of our own actions, and those of others, but of our method of thinking and arriving at any judgement.

'Such awareness requires a high level of self-analysis and self-criticism. It also demands that we are always on guard lest we drop into old habits of slothful, ill-considered thought and careless moral judgements. The pursuit of the peace of mind that flows from fulfilling our duty to our own best nature is an austere creed indeed.'

Marcus nodded. 'I agree, Doctor Galen. But how else is a man to engage with life and yet win the most permanent and precious asset he can hope to gain? As in all things, education, training and persistent practice in such a philosophical engagement with life will make the path progressively easier. It is only in the difficulty of their attainment that we establish the true worth of things.'

7

On the Pursuit
of the Virtuous Life

I T WAS HARNOUPHIS who was next to speak: 'Lord, this pursuit of a life consistent with our best nature that you describe – how is it to be accomplished?'

Marcus looked thoughtful. 'A life in pursuit of our best nature needs to be dedicated to the exercise of humanity, benevolence and justice. It demands courageous execution. If we are to practise such behaviour we need to cultivate self-control and a genuine love of truth, honesty and fair dealing. These underpin the virtuous behaviour we desire.'

Galen considered Marcus's words. 'What if a man should find that his fellow men disdain such virtues, seeing their practice as, at best, unworldly naïvety or feigned piety?'

Marcus took no offence at Galen's challenge. 'If others find his personal example good enough to emulate, so be it. But whether they find his behaviour commendable or laughable, he should adhere to the standards of conduct he has set himself as resolutely as the legionary holds his position in the line of battle.

'The judgements of others are fickle. Today's acclaimed hero will soon be cast down by public opinion as yesterday's fool or villain. The only judgement we need to consider is that of our own conscience: it is after all what the gods have given us for this very purpose. Above all, we must hold fast to the admonition: "To thine own self be true."

'If others conduct themselves badly, so be it. The condition of each man's soul is his own responsibility. You will come to grief only through failing your own test of integrity. Moreover, you should resist the temptation of paying back abuse in its own coin. You cannot win the day by casting down your own cohort's standard and taking up the flag of the enemy. To refrain from imitation is the best revenge.'[13]

Harnouphis considered Marcus's words and carefully crafted his own into a form he judged would win the Emperor's best pleasure. 'Lord, it is clear to me that you, beyond all other men, have the necessary discipline and presence of mind to achieve the excellent standards of behaviour you have described. That is surely something to be proud of, is it not?'

But Marcus responded mildly, with no glimmer of satisfaction: 'A man should exercise virtuous behaviour without ostentation or boastfulness. He should wear these behaviours naturally and unassumingly, much as he does an everyday tunic.

'Pride is an invidious threat to our moral character. It puffs us up with vanity and encourages us to conduct ourselves not in pursuit of our own best nature but to gain the flattery and approval of others. We thereby become the willing puppets of those from whom we seek approval and lose our own power of self-determination.

'Praise, or the lack of it, does nothing to add to or subtract from the essential beauty or virtue of an object. By conducting ourselves in line with our own best nature we should neither seek plaudits nor feel that we deserve them. We are merely being true to our own natures, just as the less virtuous man is to his.

'To guard against pride we should constantly remind ourselves that even the most powerful ruler occupies but a small corner of land in a world that is no more than an insignificant pin-point in the universe. Reflect also upon the brevity of our lives against the backdrop of eternity, and how we can be snatched away at any moment. Even the memories of our deeds are unlikely to survive for more than two or three generations, until these generations are themselves swept away.

'It is only by cultivating genuine humility that we can remain true to a virtuous path and capable of seeking help from others when necessary. Such help may take the form of criticism of our views. Humility teaches us how to accept such criticism kindly, in the knowledge that it serves to sharpen our own faculty of reason.'

At this point Galen intervened: 'What of our treatment of our fellow men?'

Marcus responded: 'For me it follows, as I have said, that we are duty-bound to engage in life on terms that the gods have set for us. They have granted us high intellect and those finer attributes that such intellect allows: above all, empathy for our fellow men.

'From such natural empathy flows our wish for justice, fairness, truth and benevolence for others. We hold these qualities in high regard because we know how much we ourselves appreciate them when they are granted us, and how much we grieve when they are denied us. Our empathy for our fellow man allows us to understand that denying these qualities to him, when it is in our power to grant them, would cause him suffering similar to our own. Because we empathise with him, we are forced to share his pain. Our fellow man is made of the same poor flesh and blood as us; he shares the same hopes and fears. He is deserving of our pity and our help.

'I accept that such empathy is not granted to all men in the same degree, but neither is physical strength nor wisdom. I speak here of the best quality of empathy in man, which not all will attain. And even those who do attain it may, from time to time, fail to behave in this ideal way. Such practical issues do not undermine my essential thesis, they simply demonstrate how difficult is the path we are beholden to follow.

'We also need to remind ourselves that few sane men are intentional evil-doers. And those sane men who do perpetrate evil are behaving in accordance with their own moral code and logic. If we wish to modify the actions of such men we must be able to enter into their minds and understand the rationale behind the actions of which we disapprove. Only then can we apply reasoned argument to alter their viewpoint and thus their future behaviour. If we fail in such an attempt we can only blame ourselves for our own lack of perspicuity.

'In the last analysis, men behave as they do either because it is their natures so to do or because they know no better. In either case, how can we blame someone for his nature or his ignorance?'

Harnouphis then posed another question: 'And what of the treatment that is meted out to us by the hands of the gods?'

Marcus considered briefly. 'Over the actions of the gods and blind providence we have no control. To judge such actions as good or bad is to impose moral judgements upon the earthquake, fire and flood. Such events are innocent, undeserving of the moral constructs we might falsely impose upon them. In seeing such events as deliberately seeking to injure us we become embittered for no purpose. It is better to accept such catastrophes without malice.

Only in this way can we hope to maintain the cheerful pursuit of our own best nature.

'Rather than ask the gods, "Why has this happened to me?" we should thank them for equipping us with the strength and fortitude we gain from philosophy, which enables us to bear that which the gods have chosen for us.

'We should also not fret over what the gods or providence have denied us, but rather choose to enjoy those many things that have been granted to us. However, we should not revel in the enjoyment of such gifts to the extent that their loss would deprive us of our peace of mind.'

Harnouphis posed a further question: 'But what, Lord, if fate determines that we should bear great suffering, pain or bereavement?'

Marcus responded: 'Then we should comfort ourselves that pain is a natural condition of that part of our animal being that we call our body. Pain enters our intellect and soul only with our permission. If our body suffers such pain that it is unbearable, then it brings a blessed end to us; but if it can be borne, we go on.

'It is inevitable and natural that our hearts will grieve when we suffer the loss of those that we hold dear. Such pain of the heart can far exceed that of the body. Despite Stoic teachings to the contrary, I hold that to attempt to deny such suffering is both false and pointless: the heart has its reasons of which reason knows not. Reason therefore cannot directly speak to, or assuage, the deep sufferings of the heart. However, on such painful bereavements we can still thank the gods for having first blessed us with our loved ones, and for the time they were granted to us: in this way may we yet find some degree of solace.'

It was Galen who then spoke: 'These are indeed worthy objectives you have set before us, and you have shown us the path we need to tread to reach them. But what man can aspire to conduct himself in accordance with such demanding moral precepts?'

Marcus smiled. 'My friends, every man can *aspire* to these precepts. It is in their execution that the challenge lies! We must accept that, in setting out to accomplish such high ideals, being only mortal men, from time to time we will fail to live up to our own aspirations. As on a military expedition, occasional minor defeats and setbacks are to be expected. Such setbacks should serve only to steel our resolve to return to the engagement, having gained something of value from the hard-won experience of failure. The gods will not judge us harshly for having encountered problems along the path to virtue, only for never having set out upon it, or for having surrendered at the setbacks we encountered.

'If we think that a virtuous life is possible – which it is – it behoves us to strive for it, regardless of difficulties. The ideals I have set out may be hard to achieve but our journey towards them is easily set out and easily understood:

'*To undertake our work on hand in accordance with what we know to be right, with enthusiasm, manfully and with kind-heartedness. In this pursuit we should allow no lesser issues to distract us, but instead preserve our spirit pure and upright, as if at the next moment we might have to return it Him who gave it. If we take this position firmly, expecting nothing and avoiding nothing, but instead remaining content simply that we have conducted ourselves in accordance with what we know to be right, and with truthfulness with our fellow man, then this is the path to a happy life, and there is no man or god who can prevent us from following it.*'[14]

With these words, Marcus finished his wine and stood up, addressing those present at the table: 'Come my friends, we have discussed enough this evening and our conversation has roamed over many landscapes. I believe we have acquitted ourselves well, so let us now retire for the night.'

Servants arrived to clear the table and carry the sleeping Lucius to his bedchamber. We all retired to our rooms to visit in dreams the vision of the path to the supreme good that Marcus had set before us.

8

Epilogue:
On Gods and the Hereafter

T HE DISCUSSIONS AT Aquileia took place in the
     seventh year of Marcus's reign. Twelve long years
had now passed since that happy evening on the Adriatic.
The trials that had faced Marcus in the interim were many:
the loss of his dissolute but beloved adopted brother,
Lucius – some say at the hand of a poisoner; the death of
his much-loved wife Faustina, who had borne him fourteen children; and betrayal and rebellion from his friend
Cassius, some said at the instigation of Faustina.

Worst of all was his tolerant disappointment at the
emergence of the increasingly disreputable nature of his
son Commodus. So different was Commodus from
Marcus in nature that rumour had it that Faustina had
lain with one of her favourite gladiators. All of these
setbacks Marcus had borne stoically and alone. He had
continued to serve Rome well, benevolently as a governor
and vigorously as the commander of our armies.

It was one night in Rome, many months after the flames of Marcus's funeral pyre had died down and his ashes been gathered for their final resting place of honour, that my friend the Emperor visited me one last time – in a dream. We were on a great trireme war-galley, sweeping over a mirrored sea towards the western skies as a purple evening closed around us. The dying embers of the sun settled over the western horizon and the flaming disc ahead of us sank quietly into the distant ocean.

The banks of oars slapped rhythmically into the ocean as they swept us swiftly toward the dying sun. The gentle hiss of the waves cut by our bow was broken only by the occasional cries of gulls and the random crack of the foreman's whip as he urged one or more of the galley slaves to heed the stroke-beat of his fellows. We had had a good meal with plenty of wine.

Marcus looked at me across the table as we sat in the forecastle of the ship. 'So, Rufus, my loyal Praetorian Prefect, have you struggled manfully with the classic conundrum I left you with so long ago in Aquileia?'

'I have my Lord,' I replied cheerfully. As is the nature of dreams, I was unsurprised at conversing with one long since dead; my heart was simply joyous at being once more in his company.

'And what is your answer? How can the gods be benevolent in a world in which evil falls upon good and bad alike?'

'There could be several possible answers, Lord.'

Marcus smiled. He was once more young and untroubled, and his goodness shone through to me in the gathering darkness. 'Please go on, Rufus – enlighten us.'

'The first possibility is that our understanding of good and evil is not the same as the gods' understanding of these things. While we feel that bad things happen to innocent people, perhaps in the eyes of the gods they are not so innocent. They may have done some terrible evil unbeknown to us which has earned them the gods' displeasure.'

The mischievous glint I remembered so well was in Marcus's eye as he looked at me. 'Have you ever heard of evil befalling new-born babies?'

'I have indeed, and pitiful it is.'

'And do you think it likely that, in their brief span of existence, such babes have perpetrated such great wrongs that they deserve the wrath of the gods?'

'No, but perhaps the sins of their parents or their tribe are being visited upon them?'

'But would you say that for the gods to punish an innocent in place of the guilty would be an act of benevolence?'

'Probably not, Lord.' I felt uncomfortable at how easily Marcus had dismissed the first part of my argument.

'I think I would agree with you on that, Rufus. So what do you see as another possible answer to the problem?'

'That the gods are unaware that innocents suffer great evil, my Lord.'

Marcus took a sip of wine. 'But we agreed that, for gods to deserve that title, they must be all-knowing.'

'Yes...' I saw what was coming next.

'Then how can the gods be unaware of evils that befall innocents?'

'If they are all-knowing, Lord, they cannot.'

'And if they are not all-knowing, can they be regarded as gods?'

'No, they cannot.'

'It seems we are casting away your answers in quick time, Rufus. But please go on and tell us about the other possible answers.'

'The next would be that the gods know of the evils that befall us and disapprove of them but are unable to intervene.'

'Surely by definition a god is all-powerful?'

'But gods may not all have the same power. Some, such as Jupiter, may be more powerful than others.'

'But then even the most powerful of the gods tolerates evil.'

'Yes ... I see your point ... If even the most powerful of gods contests evil but cannot prevent it, then he is not all-powerful and cannot be regarded as supreme. But there is one final possibility, Lord.'

'What is that, Rufus?'

'That the gods know of the evil that befalls innocents and have the power to intervene, but choose not to.'

Marcus looked quizzically at me. I could see we were coming to the end of this dialectical argument. 'Why would benevolent gods choose not to intervene?'

'Possibly because they have decided that man must be left to his own devices. Or because they have struck a bargain with a malign god who is to have sway over the earth for a time.'

Marcus considered this before speaking again. 'Suppose a mad galley slave were to rush up on to this deck right now and hold a knife to your throat. And suppose that I could easily wrestle your attacker to the ground but choose instead to sit and watch your throat being cut for my own amusement. Would you then say that, by failing to intervene, I have become an accomplice of this madman?'

'I suppose a court of law would see it that way.'

'So ... if the gods are aware of great evils and are able to intervene but choose, for whatever reason, not to, then they become a party to such evils?'

I felt driven back to a corner. 'Yes, Lord, according to civic law that would be the judgement.'

'If not on the basis of our own moral code, then on what grounds are we to establish the meaning of *bene-volence*? ... So, what other possibilities have you considered, Rufus?'

'None, my Lord. Those you have refuted are the only ones I could imagine.'

Marcus looked more serious. 'There *are* others, Rufus. If we discount the possibilities that the gods are not all-knowing, or are not all-powerful, or somehow are not benevolent, there yet remain further possibilities.' He paused to look at me.

The galley continued smoothly into the enveloping darkness. A myriad bright stars were appearing in the firmament.

'These being, my Lord ...?'

'Clearly the gods *could* be malevolent towards us. Or perhaps they simply don't exist in the terms we under-stand. In either case, would you say they were deserving of our worship?'

'I would say definitely not.' Yet I was shocked that a Roman emperor could even suggest that the gods were unworthy of worship. If the Emperor doubted the exist-ence of gods that could be entreated for the good of Rome, then what was left? If the gods indeed existed, malign or otherwise, would they tolerate such a belief? Mighty as the Emperor was, I half expected a bolt of lightning would strike Marcus down.

'Surely you are not suggesting that the gods do not exist?'

Marcus was smiling calmly. 'No, not that they don't exist. I am simply demonstrating, through your own logic, that it is doubtful they exist in the form we think them to exist.'

My head was spinning. All I could manage to do was re-state the question: 'Do you really believe that the gods don't exist, or that that they are malign?'

Marcus was looking at me and, in the flickering light of the deck torches, I caught the glint of his teeth in a grin. 'Rufus, do you think that any man can be certain of anything in this world?'

'Of some things I believe we can be certain. I believe I can be certain that I sit next to you on this galley and that we are sailing across this great ocean towards the distant horizon.' Such is the power of dreams. I truly believed at that moment that I was with Marcus on this great ship, sailing that dark ocean towards the setting sun.

Marcus smiled more openly at my expressed certainty, but nodded all the same. 'I see ... But of the fundamental things – such as whether the gods exist or whether our lives and the universe have an ultimate purpose – would you say that we can be truly certain?'

I shook my head. 'No, Lord, such things are outside the wisdom of men.'

'Yet, being men, and leading considered lives as the Greek philosophers exhort us to do – indeed that being the only life truly worth living – we are each obliged to take a position on such matters.'

'Not all men feel so obliged.'

'Agreed, but such men fail to grasp the very essence of life. By leading unconsidered lives we reduce ourselves to the level of simple wretches who eke out our brief spans of existence to no purpose other than to bring into this world offspring who will suffer the same fate. If a man fails to use his intellect he squanders this brief moment of eternity that he has been granted to attempt to grasp the great mystery of things. What a waste!

'Let me put it to you this way, Rufus. Although we cannot be certain of the ultimate purpose of all things, we can choose to believe, or not to believe, that such a purpose exists, can we not?'

'Yes...' I could not see where this was taking us.

'If we believe that the world and our struggles within it are merely mechanical and purposeless, we must be saying that all the efforts, tears and pain of countless generations yet to come will all eventually be nothing more than shapeless dust drifting in a void. Surely then man's position in the universe would be the cruellest of jokes? We would have been given what intellect and insight we have only to be able to grasp the meaninglessness of our own existence, the ultimate futility of all our endeavours. What value then intellect and reason? It would be as if a blind man were granted vision only to reveal to him that he had been cast perpetually into a dark, featureless terrain. In such a situation it would be better to remain blind and so blissfully unaware of one's dismal and hopeless circumstances!

'For my part, I would consider a universe with no

ultimate purpose, no great goal, a fundamental obscenity. Hence I reject the possibility.'

Marcus paused to take a drink of wine, then fell silent for a moment. I waited for him to continue.

'So you see, Rufus, I hold that we have a choice to make in life. We can choose to adopt a belief to explain those things we do not for certain know, and probably can never know, or we can simply assume that we and the universe have no purpose – in which case it must follow that our being granted the intelligence to understand all this is but a cruel joke.' He gestured dismissively with his goblet at the darkening horizon and the cosmos beyond.

'If we choose to believe that we have been placed in the world for a purpose, albeit unfathomable, we can go on to believe that this mysterious purpose is noble rather than base.'

Marcus stopped to gaze at me. When he continued his voice, though remaining calm, betrayed his deep underlying passion. 'Do you, see, Rufus, that about such profound matters we men cannot be certain. Instead we have complete freedom of belief, including the freedom not to believe at all. But taking a stand on belief is, for me, the very foundation of a considered life. On it we build our whole outlook, from it emerges our means of engagement in life and our relationship with our fellow men.

'So we come to your question. Do I really doubt the existence of the gods? Well ... there may well be higher beings out there', he raised his goblet to the now starlit sky, 'so powerful and all-knowing that beside them we are but ants. They may well live their lives on another plane, in another dimension. They may to a greater or lesser extent control our destinies – so it could indeed be wise to entreat them, in which case they may deserve the title of gods. But could any of them be the *one* supreme God? To call them this would, I believe, be inappropriate: they are still but fellow creatures in this universe.

'We men must ourselves take responsibility for those evils in the world that are man-made. We cannot blame the gods for the actions of men, or even for those of the natural world. Man's actions are our own doing. The actions of nature, on the other hand, are the actions of a world that has no concept of good or evil. The world simply is what it is. Only in their accidental collision with us do we brand natural actions as good or evil. Nature itself performs these actions innocently, with no intent either malicious or benign.

'If we say that there is some sort of *supreme God* who is all-powerful, all-knowing and essentially good, then surely what *He is* is the universe and all things, ourselves included, in its eternal journey towards its great unknowable goal, which we have to believe is both good and worthy. In such a definition, we are part of God and He is part of us, as all things are on this journey.

'In our day-to-day actions, in striving to achieve our

own best nature, we move ourselves and the universe, of which we are an infinitesimal part, to some tiny degree in the direction of the Great Goal and its intended order. Conversely, when we fail to act in accordance with our own best nature, we to some minute degree reverse the intended, natural flow of things and move them back towards the disorder from which we and all things sprang.'

Marcus paused and looked at me. 'Do you understand, Rufus?'

I nodded. Such a definition of God was metaphysical indeed, and difficult to grasp. It referred not to a being, nor even to a thing, but to a process of transition, a transformation, a positive cosmic evolution of the highest order. Marcus was right: no proof of such a God could ever be forthcoming. The concept was based on a chosen personal outlook on life: as we are part of the universe, so we have our part to play in its unfolding story, its intent, no matter how insignificant our role may be in the vastness of all creation. To expect such a God to deliver us our purposes would be to turn the whole construction the wrong way round. It is for *us* to strive to deliver, and moreover *to become*, His Great Goal, whatever that may be, through our attempts to live our brief lives according to our own best natures.

I looked at Marcus, sitting facing me, as the vessel gently rocked forwards. Somehow I now began to feel, with trepidation, that this was but a fading dream, that

these were to be my last moments together with my Lord
and friend. I had one final question to put to him before
reluctantly awaking to a day that would be darker than the
night my dream had wrapped me in.

'Lord, is this the sea of belief that even now carries your
spirit forward into the darkness, to that which lies beyond?'

Marcus smiled. In the glimmering starlight his body
now seemed insubstantial, almost translucent. I fancied I
was starting to see stars shining through the outline of his
figure.

'It is, Rufus. It is. But let us now retire. The hour is late
and it is time for me to return to the peace of that deepest
slumber that I have earned for myself. You, however, must
now go on towards the rising sun, for I am already setting.'[15]

The great troop galley glided smoothly across the placid
Mediterranean Sea which, like a mirror, reflected the dome
of stars above, stretching as far as the eye could see. It
seemed as if our ship no longer moved across an ocean of
water, but through an endless ocean of stars, above and
below. The rhythmic stroke of our oars beat a journey
across the vastness of time and space itself. And suddenly I
saw that our ship was no longer great, it was infintesimally
small against this cosmic backdrop as we made our way
towards His ultimate, unknowable, Great Goal.

APPENDIX

The Relevance of Marcus Aurelius's Beliefs to Modern Times

IN MORE RECENT history admiration for Marcus Aurelius and his beliefs has waxed and waned. He was highly considered in the latter part of the nineteenth century, his unflinching commitment to his duty to defend an empire under threat greatly appealing to late Victorians facing similar problems.

As if in direct counterpoint to this, the early twentieth century dismissed him as a 'prig', displaying a hectoring moral tone and outlook. This was grossly unfair. The *Meditations* were written solely for Marcus's own enlightenment, not for others. Moreover, it is clear from historical records and contemporary statements that Marcus not only held high moral beliefs but also put them into practice in his own life: here was no hypocrite.

Those who criticise Marcus for his moral beliefs set out in the *Meditations* are gravely at risk of finding themselves condemning the active application of moral belief itself. This is perhaps the key to the present importance of his beliefs to us. Their value is in the challenge of outlook that they throw down, echoing over the two millennia that now separate us from him, against our own set of values in the twenty-first century.

We live in a period when clever and admired satire has been used to tear down most of the conventional totems of moral guidance and authority that we inherited from the generation who fought in the Second World War. Many of these deserved to be torn down: they were already rotten examples of an outdated class system, irrational beliefs and hypocrisy. But now that we have demolished all positions of moral authority, what is left? We find ourselves in a devastated forest where all moral belief is regarded as objectively indefensible and, conversely, where amoral behaviour is seen as objectively unchallengeable.

The Church has failed to seize the initiative here and, as I have already indicated, has confused itself and others by misjudging issues of natural and personal sexual dispos-ition as vital matters of morality. In doing this the Church involves itself in controversial issues that are none of its concern, while it fails to engage in those that are central to the challenge of the age – for, in the absence of moral principles, what is left?

Issues such as honesty, justice, truth and decency have been relegated to matters of personal preference, to be espoused or ignored in much the same way as we opt for sugar in our coffee or not. Those public exemplaries who forsake these values do not hold themselves greatly accountable for their omissions, and neither do their peers demand such accountability. In consequence, the term 'honour' is no longer even worthy of satire: it is now simply too antique and quaint a concept even for ridicule.

Yet individual moral standards, and a deep-felt need to honour them, even and especially when it costs us, are the very foundations of any civilised society intent on long-term survival. Fundamentalist and fascist regimes, of the extreme left and right, of their very nature find a rational and fair moral social code an anathema. They thereby conceive the germ of their own destruction and, for that reason, cannot survive in the long term.

Today's liberal Western society is besotted with materialism. Self-seeking avarice receives authorative approval as a state creed, and so is the only basis for acceptable moral behaviour that presently exists. Yet we all recognise that the planet itself cannot sustain unrestrained personal greed into the medium term. We all know that the resources to sustain an unreservedly selfish way of life simply do not exist. Our lack of concern for the effects on future generations will create an ecological desert.

Masses of people, especially the young, wander aimlessly in a moral wilderness with no worthy examples of ethical behaviour. Even the concept of a set of rational moral codes is unknown to them, let alone the idea that a reflective life is necessary to arrive at such codes. They distract themselves with superficial entertainment and hedonistic activity to structure their time. We observe an increasing incidence of teenage pregnancies and relationship breakdowns – which result in disadvantaged children; there are more and more suicides, and prison populations of record numbers. Pushing responsibility for these matters on to faceless bureaucrats and social workers does not seem to stem the tide of advancing social breakdown.

Problems resulting from the lack of consensual individual moral beliefs cannot be resolved at the hierarchal level of society: this is simply one step too high. Change is needed within each constituent element of society – within the individual.

Imposed social structures cannot compensate for a lack of individual moral belief. The best that that can be hoped for is that the most extreme forms of antisocial behaviour will be constrained. However, because such constraints are imposed without moral justification from above, they generate further tensions and resistance in those sections of society which already consider themselves marginalised.

If we fail to re-establish a set of consensual moral precepts our society runs the real risk of degenerating into a last-stand, Big Brother police state. A primitive degree of social order can then be delivered only by being imposed from above, with no consensual moral justification, and thereby necessarily oppressing our hard-won prizes of justice, free speech and democracy.

Playing mind-games of 'Ain't it awful?' with each other may gel relationships between like-minded, readily scandalised, mature citizens but they do nothing to reverse the situation. Fundamental resolution of the social and ecological threats that presently face us can be delivered only if society – no matter how multi-cultural in composition – is based on a single set of consensual moral beliefs.

Such moral beliefs largely need to be rebuilt from the ground up. Today's system of ethics cannot be based upon a bygone acceptance of class conformity, mono-ethnic cultural values, 'respect for one's betters', unhealthy obsessions with particular sexual practices or unchallengeable religious dogma. We live in a pluralistic, intellectually critical and rightly challenging age.

We need to seek consensus around a set of life-affirming moral beliefs that are robust enough to withstand the rigour of reasoned debate. They need to be based on rational precepts that take their authority from what is not simply best for ourselves but best also for other people, and for our children and our children's children.

Marcus's set of classical beliefs offers our present age one visible beacon of moral principle founded on rational thinking. Given the exhaustive 'field-trial' of these beliefs – they held at least one man together through a veritable hailstorm of adversity – I would suggest that even today, perhaps especially today, almost two millennia later,

Marcus's beliefs warrant at least a cursory examination by anyone intent on pursuing a 'reflective life' and searching for a moral anchor.

REFERENCES

1 *Marcus Aurelius: A Biography*, Anthony R. Birley, 2000, Routledge, London, p.222.

2 *Marcus Aurelius: Meditations*, translated by Maxwell Staniforth, 1964, Penguin Books Ltd, London, p.29.

3 *Ibid*. p.115.

4 Anthony R. Birley, *op. cit*. p.38.

5 *Ibid*. p.159.

6 *Ibid*. p.164.

7 *Ibid*. p.206.

8 *Ibid*. p.198.

9 Maxwell Staniforth, *op. cit*. p.20.

10 *Ibid*. p.115.

11 Anthony R. Birley, *op. cit*. p.223.

12 Maxwell Staniforth, *op. cit*. p.21.

13 *Ibid*. p.91.

14 Anthony R. Birley, *op. cit*. p.222.

15 *Ibid*. p.210.

ACKNOWLEDGEMENTS

The author gratefully acknowledges permission to quote from the Penguin Group for passages from *Marcus Aurelius: Meditations* translated by Maxwell Staniforth (Penguin Classics, 1964), copyright Maxwell Staniforth, 1964, and from Routledge for passages from *Marcus Aurelius: A Biography* by Anthony R. Birley, published 2000. The passages are identified in the References.

FURTHER READING

Marcus Aurelius: Meditations, translated by Maxwell Staniforth, Penguin Books, London, 1964.

The Climax of Rome, Michael Grant, Readers Union, Weidenfeld & Nicolson, London, 1969.

Marcus Aurelius: A Biography, Anthony R. Birley, Routledge, London, 2000.